Christ's Mother & Ours

OTHER BOOKS BY OSCAR LUKEFAHR, C.M.

"We Believe..."
A Survey of the Catholic Faith

A Catholic Guide to the Bible

The Privilege of Being Catholic

The Catechism Handbook

Workbooks also available

Christ's Mother & Ours

A CATHOLIC GUIDE TO MARY

Father Oscar Lukefahr, C.M.

Liguori
ONE LIGUORI DRIVE
LIGUORI MO 63057-9999
314.464.2500

Imprimi Potest:
James Shea, C.SS.R.
Provincial, St. Louis Province
The Redemptorists

Imprimatur:
+ Paul Zipfel, V.G.
Auxiliary Bishop, Archdiocese of St. Louis

ISBN 0-7648-0214-3
Library of Congress Catalog Card Number: 98-65699

This book was previously published under the title *Morning Star*, ©
1995, Liguori Publications.

Cover design by Grady Gunter

DEDICATION

To Mary
And to All
Who Have Taught Me to Love Her

CONTENTS

INTRODUCTION

A young woman rang our doorbell and asked to speak to a priest. She was carrying a Bible and seemed anxious. Tears came into her eyes as she explained that the pastor of her non-denominational church had announced that the world would end in the year 2000. The Book of Revelation, he had assured the congregation, pointed out 2000 as the year when Jesus would come upon the clouds to destroy evildoers and bring his elect to heaven.

I talked with the young woman for quite some time. I told her that the Book of Revelation gives no timetable for the end of the world. Jesus himself said, "But of that day or hour, no one knows...only the Father" (Mark 13:32). Down through the centuries various groups have tried to predict the time of the end of the world. They've all been wrong! Besides, this world ends for each one of us the moment we die, and we need to rely on the compassion of Christ to bring us to eternal life.

The young woman seemed somewhat reassured by our conversation, but her experience shows that much current speculation about the year 2000 engenders confusion and fear. A better approach is indicated by Pope John Paul II in his encyclical letter, *Mother of the Redeemer:* "...the Bimillennial Jubilee of the Birth of Jesus Christ...directs our gaze towards his Mother" (# 3).

Mary was the first to know of the coming birth of Jesus two thousand years ago. She was the "Morning Star" who heralded the coming of the "Sun of Justice," Jesus Christ. Today she will guide us from the darkness of fear and anxiety to the light of truth and hope. She can help us usher in the year 2000—a special birthday celebration for Jesus—with serenity and joy. As the third millennium approaches, we are invited to imitate Mary as she reflected on the events of Christ's birth and "pondered them in her heart" (Luke 2:19).

That is the purpose of this book, to view Mary as the one who announces the presence of Jesus Christ as the Son of God and Savior of humankind. In recent years, there have been many indications that Mary is making special efforts to bring the world to Jesus. The Second Vatican Council spotlighted Mary's role as Mother of the Church. Recent popes have written encyclical letters about Mary. Theologians of many denominations have published books on the importance of Mary to all Christians. There have been reports that Mary has been appearing in various parts of the world, and media investigations into such appearances have presented them in a positive light. Millions have made pilgrimages to approved shrines, such as those at Fatima and Lourdes. Mary is news!

And she should be. The Catholic Church has always honored Mary, and Catholics believe that true devotion to Mary will bring people closer to her son. The more the world knows about Mary, the more the world will come to know Jesus Christ.

In this book we will reflect on the place Mary has in Catholicism (Chapter 1), a place marked out in the Scriptures (Chapters 2–3), in Church teaching (Chapter 4), in the liturgy (Chapter 5), and in apparitions (Chapter 6). We will study Mary's place in sacramentals, the arts, and life (Chapter 7). We will view Mary as a model of response to Jesus for individuals (Chapter 8) and for the family (Chapter 9). We will see how the life, death, and resurrection of Jesus can become more a part of our lives as we "translate the Bible into prayer" through Mary's rosary (Chapters 10–12).

My prayer is that Mary will be for all of us a Mother who opens our eyes and hearts to her son, Jesus Christ.

Fr. Oscar Lukefahr, C.M.

P.S. Thanks to all who helped in the writing of this book... To Sue Schuster and Father Robert Pagliari, editors for the project. To Cecelia Portlock, Kasey Nugent, and Kass Dotterweich for editing assistance. To Grady Gunter for designing the cover. To Father Arthur Trapp, C.M., who read the entire manuscript and gave valuable advice and encouragement. To Father Charles Shelby, C.M., who gave me the idea of writing this book on Mary. To Sister Nanette Durham, O.SS.R., who seconded the idea. To those who read the manuscript, answered the workbook questions, and made many valuable suggestions: Carol and Paul Berens, Bill Hopkins, Pat and Lenny Kuper, Delores Lindhurst, Joan Ruhl, and Kathy and Den Vollink. To others who helped on various stages of the project: Father Tony Falanga, Jeanne and Henry Moreno, Sallie and Rob Hurley, Guy and Millie Sextro, Anne and Chris Smith, and Kathy and Brock Whittenberger. Finally, to the class at Saint Vincent de Paul Parish in Perryville, Missouri, who once again kept me writing on schedule, and to my sister, Joann Lukefahr, D.C., who made arrangements for the class. May God bless you all and may Mary watch over you!

CHAPTER 1

WHY MARY?

When Patty was fifteen years old, her mother died suddenly. Not long after her mother's funeral, Patty went to the parish church, knelt down before a statue of Mary and said, "From now on, you will be my Mother." That was more than twenty years ago. Today Patty is married, the mother of three children. She still has a great love of Mary, and she has taught her children that Mary is their Mother too....

Katherine had a deep devotion to Mary. She prayed the rosary daily and turned to Mary in time of need, perhaps because she felt a special kinship with Mary. Katherine, like Mary, was a wife and mother. Like Mary, she suffered through the death of a son who gave his life for others. Like Mary, she lived for years as a widow. Just before she died, Katherine called on Mary for help, and I'm sure Mary was there to escort her into the presence of Jesus and to reunite Katherine with her husband and son....

Sarah was born with birth defects which kept her from taking food properly. She endured several difficult surgeries but remained a cheerful little girl who touched the hearts of all who knew her. On Mother's Day, shortly before her death, the four-year-old asked her mother to take her to the church. She knelt down before a statue of Mary. "God bless Mommy, God bless Daddy..." she prayed, and she thanked God for birds and flowers and other gifts. Then she looked up at Mary's statue, smiled, and said, "Happy Mother's Day, Mary!" Less than a month later, Sarah was with Mary, her Mother, in heaven....

My own affection for Mary goes back to my childhood. My mother taught me the Hail Mary not long after I learned to talk, and our family prayed the rosary frequently (though many times I was no model of devotion). The Catholic Church in my hometown was named in honor of Mary's Assumption. The Vincentian Community, to which I belong as a Catholic priest, is especially devoted to Our Lady of the Miraculous Medal....

All of us who have ever knelt before a statue of the Blessed Virgin or whispered a prayer to our Lady have a story to tell about why Mary, the Mother of Jesus, is our Mother too. But whether that story is Patty's, Katherine's, Sarah's, mine...or yours, we came to know Mary, our Mother, as someone who was always there for us. We took her hand as naturally as any child takes the hand of a mother.

For two thousand years, since the Child at Nazareth took the hand of his Mother, since the beloved disciple took Mary's hand as they stood beneath the cross of her son, believers have felt in Mary's touch the assurance of a mother's love. Catholics have honored Mary as Mother so fervently that today a statue of Mary in the front yard or a rosary in one's hand identifies the owner as a Catholic.

Some who are not Catholic find it hard to understand why Catholics honor Mary. At times, Catholics are criticized for their devotion to Mary. "Why pray to Mary?" we are asked. "Why not go directly to Jesus?" The first answer to such questions may be found in our vision of life.

MARY AND THE CATHOLIC FAITH

When we Catholics look at the big picture, at how we view life's meaning, we find that Mary's role is important. Catholicism is a religion which believes in God as a Trinity of Persons—Father, Son, and Holy Spirit. God is the "Supreme Being," uncreated, always existing, infinite, and perfect. Catholics believe that God made the universe, and that God's creation is "very good" (Genesis 1:31). God gave humanity a special place on earth, making us "in the image of God" (Genesis 1:27) and endowing us with intellect, will, and emotions. Made in God's image, human beings could freely choose to receive

God's love and offer that love to one another. God pointed out that whatever made this possible was good, and that whatever might cut humanity off from God's love was evil.

However, the first human beings misused their freedom. Instead of accepting God's design, they claimed the right to decide what was good and what was evil. They turned away from God in disobedience (which we call sin). As a result, humanity was weakened by a condition known as original sin. We sank into a pattern of failure and evil, changing God's paradise into a world hopelessly immersed in sin and death.

It was a situation we could not remedy. Finite human beings could not atone for the insult of sin against an infinite Being. The love relationship between God and us could be restored only if God reached down to us. And God, out of compassion and love, did reach down by offering forgiveness. Many responded to God's offer. Above all, a family of people, the Jews (also known as Hebrews or Israelites), put their faith in God. They accepted God's love in a "covenant," an agreement to be God's people. They hoped for a "new covenant" of love between God and humanity. This new covenant, they believed, would be established by a savior, a "Messiah," one anointed by God to lead humanity to its true destiny (*Catechism of the Catholic Church*, Paragraphs 198-421; quotes from the *Catechism* will henceforth be cited as C 198-421).

This covenant was formed in a way beyond imagining. God entered history by becoming one of us. The second Person of the Trinity, the Son, took on a body in the mystery we call the Incarnation. "In the beginning was the Word…and the Word was God…. And the Word became flesh" (John 1:1,14). Jesus Christ was born into our world in the little town of Bethlehem in Judea. He is divine because he is the Son of God, human because he is the Son of Mary, a Jewish girl chosen by God to be Christ's Mother.

Jesus was the Messiah hoped for by the Jews, but he far exceeded their expectations. He was more than a great king or powerful leader. Jesus was Lord and God (John 20:28). In Jesus Christ, human beings could look upon the face of God, hear God's voice, and hold God's hand. In Jesus Christ, the love of

God touched sinful humanity in an embrace of forgiveness and healing.

But evil still existed, and evil has always lashed out against the love of God. When God became human, evil found a target, for Jesus had made himself vulnerable, liable to suffering and death. Enemies quickly gathered around him and for many reasons decided that Jesus had to be eliminated.

Jesus could have used his divine power to crush his foes, but he had come to bring mercy to all, even his enemies. He refused to use force against them, relying only on love to call them to repentance. He accepted the fact that if he continued to love his enemies, he would have to love them even to death.

It was this love of Jesus Christ that saved us, an act of divine love made visible when Jesus was tortured and put to death on the cross. "No one has greater love than this, to lay down one's life for one's friends" (John 15:13).

But death could not destroy the Son of God. It could only transform the mortal body of Jesus into a glorified, immortal body. Jesus Christ passed through death so that his body was freed from the limits of space and time. On Easter Sunday, Christ appeared to his followers so gloriously alive that even the most skeptical of them worshiped him with the words, "My Lord and my God" (John 20:28). Christ formed his followers into a Church, a community of believers through which he would remain in the world. He promised that those who put their faith in him will be brought through death to eternal life. There, in God's presence and in the company of all who love God, our hearts will at last find the peace and joy for which we long.

Christ's life, death, and resurrection allow every human being to overcome the chains of sin and to dwell in God's love. What Christ has done for us is called Redemption, but Christ does not force anyone to accept it. He invites us to receive a sharing in God's life (sanctifying grace). He offers us every possible help (actual grace). When we respond by putting our faith in him and choosing to do God's will, we find salvation, our destiny of union with God (C 422–682).

As we follow Christ, we do not walk alone. Just as God formed the Jews into a family through the Old Covenant, so in the New Covenant Jesus forms us into the Church, a family of believers. In the Church, we are called to share the Good News of Jesus and to help one another. Christ acts through his Church, guiding us through its leaders and instructing us through the inspired words of the Bible. He touches believers through signs known as the sacraments, assisting us today just as he helped people during his mortal life.

Because people are free they can reject God. We live in a world where for hundreds of thousands of years people have been making choices, many of them bad. As a result, humanity suffers from war, crime, disease, poverty, famine, failure, and death. But because Christ faced and conquered these evils, we trust that we can prevail over them as well. We may not completely understand human suffering, but we know that it does not separate us from God's love and that it can be overcome. "If God is for us, who is against us?...Neither death, nor life...nor anything else in all creation, will be able to separate us from the love of God in Christ Jesus our Lord" (Romans 8:31,38-39).

The Church will last until the end of time. Christ will be with us "always, to the end of the age" (Matthew 28:20). Finally, when God's purposes are accomplished, time, as we know it, shall cease and Jesus will bring this world's history to a close in the Final Judgment. Then the full meaning of our lives will be brought to light. All who are united with God will at last be able to appreciate the grandeur of God's design, brought to completion in a masterpiece of love and beauty which Scripture calls "a new heaven and a new earth" (Revelation 21:1) (C 683–1060).

This is the Catholic vision of life, drawn from the teaching and life of Jesus Christ. Mary's place in it is both essential and unique. She stands precisely at the focal point of human history. She was one of those who lived before Christ and hoped for the Messiah. She was the first person to accept Jesus Christ in faith and to welcome him into human existence. Because Jesus was miraculously conceived in Mary's womb by God's power, she is the only person through whom Jesus Christ is related to us and to the rest of the human race.

God chose Mary, therefore, for the most important role in history after that of Jesus. Her obedience to God and her dedication to Jesus set her above all others. It is true, of course, that Mary *could not* have become the Mother of Christ without the grace of God. But God depended on Mary's consent to the Incarnation, and without Mary's faithful obedience, Christ *would not* have entered our history as he did. So the first reason Catholics honor Mary is that she played the most important part in God's plan to bring Jesus Christ into the world (C 484–511).

MARY AND THE SACRAMENTAL PRINCIPLE

A second reason Catholics pray to Mary and honor her is based on the "sacramental principle." A sacrament is a sign, and we believe that the good things God has created are sacraments, signs telling us about God. We affirm that God comes to us in the beauty of nature and in people. We believe this because God made the universe very good and because, when evil came into the world through human sinfulness, God redeemed us from sin's destruction by the life, death, and resurrection of Jesus Christ (Galatians 4:4-5). We believe that Jesus, by assuming a human body and becoming part of the physical world (1 John 1:1-2), began a process that will renew the universe (Romans 8:20-21).

The Catholic perception of God's creation and Christ's redemptive act has formed us into a community of believers who understand God in a unique way. This understanding is what we call the sacramental principle. It states that God is present in the world, disclosing God's very Self in and through creation. It declares that things, events, and people teach us about God and lead us to God. It has had a profound effect on the way we view God, the universe, and people—including Mary, the Mother of Jesus. (For a more thorough explanation of this principle and its implications, see *The Privilege of Being Catholic,* by Father Oscar Lukefahr, Liguori Publications, 1993.)

Because we Catholics believe in the goodness of people, we

trust that others on earth are signs to us of God's love. We are confident that when we are near the saints, those who have died in the love of Christ, we are in the presence of God. Above all, we are certain that Mary, who brought Jesus into the world at Bethlehem, brings him into our lives today.

Those who criticize Catholics for our devotion to Mary and the saints apparently cannot accept the sacramental principle. They see Mary and the saints as obstacles that get between us and Jesus. Their questions "Why pray to Mary? Why not go directly to Jesus?" imply that people *hinder* our efforts to follow Christ. We who are Catholic believe instead that the goodness in people directs us to God, the Source of all good.

This is God's plan, as we see in the Bible teaching about the Church as the Body of Christ. After his death and resurrection, Christ formed the community of believers into a sign of his continuing presence on earth. He said, "For where two or three are gathered in my name, I am there among them" (Matthew 18:20). When Paul was persecuting Christians, Christ asked him, "Why do you persecute me?" (Acts 9:4) This helped Paul to understand the unity between Christ and believers. He later wrote to them, "You are the body of Christ" (1 Corinthians 12:27), and explained that Christ is the head of his body, the Church (Colossians 1:18).

Jesus is not in competition with those who believe in him! As a matter of fact, Jesus depends upon his followers to continue his physical presence on earth. What is more, Jesus depends on his followers to manifest God's goodness in ways that he could not. Jesus is God, but he accepted human limitations. Since he died on the cross, he could not show how God's patience might be manifested in an elderly person. Because he remained single, he could not exemplify how God's parental care might be modeled in a parent. Because he ascended into heaven, he does not relate to our physical existence in his mortal body in the twentieth century.

But Jesus, whose body is now glorious and immortal, lives on earth in the members of his Church: the elderly, those who are parents, and people in every possible circumstance of life. "The gifts he gave were that some would be apostles, some prophets, some evangelists, some pastors and teachers, to equip the saints for the work of ministry, for building up the body of Christ, until all of us come to the unity of the faith and of the knowledge of the Son of God, to maturity, to the measure of the full stature of Christ" (Ephesians 4:11-13). Jesus invites all to be signs of God's grace and goodness, to be "Christ" to the world.

This is an essential element of our awareness of Jesus and of his influence on our lives. We can *read* about the love of Jesus in the gospels, but we *experience* it in the love of family and friends. Children encounter the forgiveness of Jesus when parents forgive them. The sick feel the healing touch of Jesus in the solicitude of doctors and nurses. Catholics recognize the teaching authority of Jesus in the pope and the holiness of Jesus in people who are truly good.

Most Catholics come to know Christ to some extent in this way. Many converts have said that they found Jesus in the example of neighbors, friends, or coworkers. Preachers and writers of many denominations often describe how Christlike virtues are brought to life in our day by saintly individuals (C 774–776, 1667–1670).

MARY, A SIGN OF GOD'S GOODNESS AND LOVE

Since Christ wants believers to reflect and embody various aspects of God's perfection, he surely expects us to look to Mary as a special sign of God's goodness. God esteemed Mary highly enough to select her as the Mother of Christ; by this choice God placed her before us as a preeminent sign of divine love.

Mary was first to know Christ and to be redeemed by his grace. She shows us what it means to accept salvation. (Christ cannot portray what it means to be saved: he is the Savior!)

As a woman, Mary can personify qualities that a man cannot. Mary as virgin daughter, mother, and wife can give us a perspective on the greatness of God that we will find nowhere else.

God, of course, transcends our designations of male and female. However, masculine and feminine qualities in human beings come from God. "So God created humankind in his image, in the image of God he created them; male and female he created them" (Genesis 1:27). Creation is like a prism which takes light and refracts it into many colors. The totality of light cannot be seen unless all the various colors are examined. So, too, we cannot appreciate the magnificence of God unless we learn to marvel at the many ways in which God's infinite goodness is reflected in creation. In particular, we cannot appreciate the manner in which God relates to us unless we study how God is "imaged" in both male and female (C 370).

Because Mary is a woman, she models those aspects of God's goodness which we usually recognize as feminine. God is always addressed as "Father" rather than "Mother" in the Bible, but both paternal and maternal roles are ascribed to God. For example, Deuteronomy 32:18 states that God (like a father) begets and (like a mother) gives birth to Israel. In Isaiah 66:13, God addresses Israel: "As a mother comforts her child, / so I will comfort you." Jesus compares himself to a mother hen protecting her chicks under her wings (Luke 13:34). So Scripture uses images which assign feminine characteristics to God in both the Old and New Testaments. These images find their finest expression in Mary.

Mary, the "virgin-handmaid" of the Lord, portrays trust and humble submission to God. Mary, the Madonna, cradling the baby Jesus in her arms, depicts God's loving tenderness. Mary, the "Pietà," receiving the broken body of Christ from the cross, personifies compassion and hope. These and countless other images of Mary have put the human family in touch with God in unique and powerful ways. They have inspired masterpieces in art, music, and literature. They have taught the world of God's limitless love for people. They have helped millions of Christians to put faith and hope in Mary's son (C 829).

MARY, A MOTHER LEADING US TO JESUS

The questions "Why pray to Mary? Why not go directly to Jesus?" suggest that we must approach God as solitary individuals and that each person stands alone before God. We who are Catholic do pray directly to Jesus. But we know that we pray as members of a family of believers. We realize that we are "citizens with the saints and also members of the household of God, built upon the foundation of the apostles and prophets, with Christ Jesus himself as the cornerstone" (Ephesians 2:19).

Catholics believe in the communion of saints, the company of those united in Christ on earth, in purgatory, and in heaven. We believe that it is God's plan to "gather up all things in him, things in heaven and things on earth" (Ephesians 1:10), to bring about a community of those who dwell in this world and in the next.

Community is essential to us as human beings. We know how important it is to have friends. Companions, relatives, and friends are blessings that bring warmth and happiness into our lives. They share our joys and help us endure our sufferings.

An example of the difference family and friends can make is the case of two children with the same illness in adjoining hospital rooms. Both receive exactly the same medical treatment. But one is alone, with no visitors and no encouragement from family and friends. The other has a mother who stays in the room, plenty of visitors, gifts of flowers on the bedside table, and greeting cards in the mail. The second child is almost certain to recover more quickly. When we consider this example, we can easily see how the knowledge that Mother Mary is nearby and that we are supported by a heavenly family of friends who can only help us in our efforts to follow Christ.

The Bible teaches that we do have friends, relatives, and companions in heaven who provide us with inspiration and love. The Letter to the Hebrews compares life to a race we are running. Victors from the past, the saints, are in the stands cheering us on. "Therefore, since we are surrounded by so great a cloud of witnesses, let us also lay aside every weight and the sin that clings so closely, and let us run with perseverance the race that is set before us, looking to Jesus the pioneer and perfecter of our faith" (12:1-2). Mary is in this cloud of witnesses; she helps us to persevere in running our race and to keep our eyes fixed on Jesus (C 963–966).

MARY, A MOTHER
WHO OPENS US TO GOD'S GRACE

A sports writer interviewing the football coach at Notre Dame University asked, "Coach, is it true that you say a prayer with your football team before every game?" "Yes, it is," replied the coach. "Now, Coach," rejoined the writer, "you don't think almighty God cares whether the Notre Dame football team wins or loses, do you?" "No," the coach said. "Almighty God doesn't care whether Notre Dame wins or loses.... But his Mother does!"

That's a funny remark, but it might be misleading. It might imply that Mary "fills in" where God is unwilling to act or that she must convince God in situations where God is reluctant to help. But God does not need a substitute and does not have to be convinced. God knows and wants what is best for us in every circumstance. The real problem is that we may be prevented from receiving what God wants because we do not recognize God's will or because our sins and those of others hinder us. Mary helps us in that she opens us to God's will and makes us more receptive to God's grace.

The Bible indicates that we should request the prayers of others and that we are helped by them. Paul asked believers to pray for him (Colossians 4:3; 1 Thessalonians 5:25). Paul prayed directly to God, but he also felt that it was important to have others praying with him and for him. If it is good to pray with others on earth and to ask them to pray for us, then it is even better to pray with the Mother of Christ and to ask her to pray for us. And the Bible indicates that the saints are united to us in prayer. The Book of Revelation pictures those in heaven as offering to God the prayers of God's people on earth (called "the saints," or "holy ones," in the New Testament): "...the twenty-four elders fell before the Lamb, each holding a harp and golden bowls filled with incense, which are the prayers of the saints" (5:8).

It must be noted that we do not pray to God and to Mary in the same way. We pray to God as the Source of all blessings. We pray to Mary in the sense that we ask her to pray with us and for us (C 2679), to be near us in love and friendship, and to lead us closer to Jesus. This is illustrated in two prayers frequently said by Catholics. In the Lord's Prayer, we ask God for what only God can give: "Give us this day our daily bread; and forgive us our trespasses." In the Hail Mary, we ask Mary to "pray for us sinners" (C 967–970, 2673–2679).

MARY, A MODEL TO BE IMITATED

Sometimes Catholics are criticized for "worshiping" Mary because we display statues and paintings of Mary and pray before those images. We do not, of course, "worship" Mary. *Worship* and *adoration* are terms that refer to the act of acknowledging God as the Supreme Being. We Catholics worship and adore God alone. But we do honor Mary.

The Bible teaches us to do this when it says that "all generations" will call Mary blessed (Luke 1:48). The Bible honors heroes and heroines of Old and New Testament times, in some cases with entire books like those of Ruth, Judith, and Esther. We emulate the Bible when we memorialize and honor Mary in word and song, in marble, stained glass, and canvas.

Most Christians erect statues of Mary…at Christmastime when they put up nativity scenes. We who are Catholic, however, do not reserve the practice to Christmas. What's more, there is nothing unusual about keeping statues and paintings in prominent places; almost any city has its statues of famous leaders and citizens. Surely there ought to be images of Mary, the greatest woman who ever lived.

At times, Catholics may seem overly enthusiastic in their devotion to Mary. But if we consider the kind of adulation commonly paid to movie stars, sports figures, and singers, we will probably have to admit that Mary comes in "second-best." The real problem is not that we honor Mary too much, but that we honor her too little.

Human beings will have their heroes and heroines, one way or another. But if we are given only secular models to emulate and follow, we will be denied the one model who can best guide us to Jesus—his Mother, Mary (C 971).

WHAT DOES CHRIST WANT?

Does Jesus want us to be aware of his Mother, to honor her, and to talk to her in prayer? If the answer to this question is yes, then we have the finest possible reason for devotion to Mary. This is what Jesus wants.

If we could go back two thousand years and visit Jesus and Mary in their home at Nazareth, would Jesus ask us to ignore Mary? Obviously not. Jesus would want us to visit with Mary, and she would inspire us to love Jesus more. Mary is close to Jesus in heaven today, and Jesus undoubtedly wants us to visit with her.

Further insight can be gained by asking, "Are we pleased when others honor our mother?" When I was pastor of Most Precious Blood Church in Denver, I invited my mother for a visit to celebrate her eightieth birthday. My friends in the parish treated her royally with flowers, dinners, birthday cakes, and congratulations. My mother was delighted, and so was I. We rejoice when others honor our mother. We can be certain that Jesus does too.

PATTY, KATHERINE, SARAH, YOU, AND I...

For Patty, Katherine, and Sarah, for me and countless others, Mary has been a Mother who has helped us to know and love Jesus more. As Mother of the Redeemer, she brought Jesus into the world. She has been bringing him into the hearts of her children ever since.

In this chapter, we have examined some of the reasons why. In God's plan for humanity, Mary was asked to accept the incredible responsibility of being Mother of the Savior. She embodies God's goodness in unique and beautiful ways. As a member of our family of believers, she is a Mother who helps us love and follow Christ. When we pray to her, she opens us to God's grace and assistance. She is a model for our imitation, a model of devotion and fidelity to her son. Finally, Christ certainly wants us to honor his Mother, for he must be as pleased as any one of us is when our mother is honored and loved.

THE BIBLE AND MARY

Many years ago, I read a comment by a Protestant theologian: "If the Bible says that all generations will call Mary blessed, then why shouldn't we?" A good question! And a good reason for moving to a study of what the Bible says about Mary, our goal in the next two chapters.

Questions for Discussion and Reflection

Think of the "story" you have to tell about how you came to love Mary. Write this story down and talk to Mary about it. If you are studying this book in a group, share your story with the members, and listen to theirs. Or do the same with a good friend.

Has your devotion to Mary increased your love for Jesus? Would your life be richer or poorer without devotion to Mary? Does this help explain why Catholics honor Mary?

In your own prayer, what are some of the differences between your worship (adoration) of God and the honor you give Mary?

Who are some of the famous people (rock stars and movie actors and actresses) who are "idolized" today? In what sense are these people heroes and heroines? In what sense is Mary a heroine, and how can remembering and honoring her make us better human beings and more faithful followers of Christ?

Activities

In your own words, write a brief explanation for each of the following terms: *God, creation, sin, covenant, Messiah, Incarnation, Redemption, Church, sanctifying grace, actual grace, the sacramental principle, communion of saints, worship and adoration, prayer to God, prayer to Mary.*

Pray the Our Father slowly and reverently. Then pray the Hail Mary. Ask Mary to help you love God as she does.

Hail Mary

Hail Mary, full of grace. The Lord is with thee. Blessed art thou among women, and blessed is the fruit of thy womb, Jesus. Holy Mary, Mother of God, pray for us sinners, now and at the hour of our death. Amen.

WHAT THE NEW TESTAMENT SAYS ABOUT MARY

"I don't understand how you Catholics can believe that Mary prays for us," a young man remarked to me, "when the Bible says that the dead don't know anything. As far as I am concerned, Ecclesiastes 9:5 settles the issue."

This statement was made in good faith, I'm sure, but it is a classic example of how to *mis*use the Bible. Ecclesiastes 9:5 declares: "The living know that they will die, but the dead know nothing." The young man took this passage as the only word of the Bible on life after death. He placed the author of Ecclesiastes on the same level as Jesus! He focused narrowly on one passage of the Bible and neglected many others.

UNDERSTANDING THE BIBLE: ORIGINS AND INTERPRETATION

This incident sheds light on an important fact as we study Mary in the Bible. To understand what the Bible teaches about a given topic, we must be familiar with the whole Bible, its nature and its message.

The Bible came to us through a complex process involving God's interaction with many generations of human beings. A collection of books, the Bible is divided into the Old Testament, written before Jesus Christ over a period of more than a thousand years, and the New Testament, written during the one hundred years after Christ's Resurrection.

The Church, under God's guidance, decided which books belonged in the Bible. By A.D. 125, many writings about Jesus, including all of those now found in the New Testament, were being circulated among Christians. Some were regarded as authoritative because of their apostolic origins and doctrinal content. Some were rejected. By the end of the fourth century, there was a general consensus among Christians that the Bible should contain the forty-six Old Testament books and the twenty-seven New Testament books now found in the Catholic Bible. This consensus was expressed in Church councils, like those at Rome in 382, Hippo in 393, and Carthage in 397.

The Church chose these books because it believed they were inspired by God. "All scripture is inspired by God and is useful for teaching, for reproof, for correction, and for training in righteousness" (2 Timothy 3:16; see also 2 Peter 1:20-21). The exact nature of inspiration is not explained in Scripture, and the way people perceive inspiration is likely to color the way they understand the Bible.

Some Christians contend that inspiration means God's dictation of the Bible to human beings, who merely recorded what God said. They interpret the Bible in a "fundamentalist" way, holding that the words must be understood according to their face value. They tend to view passages in isolation, to see them all as equal, and to say that there can be no flaw of any kind in the Bible.

In the Catholic understanding of inspiration, God did not merely dictate words but influenced the authors to use their own talents and abilities. As a result, the Bible is both the Word of God and the work of human beings. Since this is so, we must know something about the human authors, their lives and times, and the styles and literary forms they used if we want to understand the Bible.

Because this approach emphasizes that we must study the "context" of each writing, it leads to a method of interpretation called contextual. This method stresses the importance of viewing each passage in the light of the whole Bible. It holds that the truths which God inspired for our salvation are without error, but that the Bible has limitations which come from its human origins. Among these limitations is the way we human beings must learn things step by step. From ignorance, we move progressively toward knowledge and wisdom.

Authors of the Old Testament books were unaware of many truths later revealed by Jesus, and Jesus had to refine and develop their teaching in many ways (Matthew 5:17-48). Even after Jesus, Christians came only gradually to the full meaning of what Christ had taught. At first, for instance, many Christians thought that they had to observe all Jewish regulations. Later, they realized that Christ had nullified these restrictions and so they maintained only a few directives for the sake of good order (Acts 15). Finally, they understood that all such mandates were a thing of the past. So as the Holy Spirit guided the inspired writers of both Old and New Testaments, they came to a clearer understanding of God's truth.

From this we can see how important it is to know the origin and background of biblical books. Since the Holy Spirit progressively guides the Church to a fuller understanding of the truth (John 16:13), learning when and how each book was written can teach the "direction" the Holy Spirit is marking out for us.

Thus the author of Ecclesiastes, who wrote three hundred years before Christ, was unaware of eternal life. Later Old Testament books, such as 1 and 2 Maccabees and Wisdom, taught the existence of life after death. Jesus made the reality of eternal life absolutely clear, and his teaching is proclaimed throughout the New Testament. So the gentleman who quoted Ecclesiastes to prove that Mary cannot hear our prayers was "behind the times." Using Ecclesiastes to understand eternal life is like using a map drawn by Christopher Columbus to get from New York to Los Angeles!

"A CONVERSATION
YOU MIGHT HEAR IN HEAVEN"

"If only we'd had cassette recorders and computers in our day," exclaimed Mark. "What a book we could have written!" "Well, we didn't have them, so there's no use dreaming," replied John. "And don't forget, we *did* help produce the greatest bestseller of all time." "That's true," said Mark, "but I would still like to go back and change a few things." "Don't be too hard on yourself," counseled Luke. "You didn't have much time, and you were busy dodging those Romans. The believers were discouraged by persecution and misunderstanding, and you had to help them realize that Jesus was persecuted and misunderstood too." "That's so," admitted Mark, "and that's why I emphasized all those episodes from the Lord's life where he was misunderstood. But why did I have to make it look like Mary didn't believe in her own son? I feel like blushing every time I see her. Good thing she has such a sense of humor. She just laughs and says that my writing made you and Matthew and John think more deeply about her place in God's plan." "Exactly," chimed in Matthew. "If you hadn't paved the way, we wouldn't have been able to plan our gospels so carefully. We had more time than you did, and it takes time for inspiration to sink in. And forget about cassette recorders and computers. If they'd been around two thousand years ago, our gospels would be so long no one would read them!"

Whether the evangelists have ever had such a conversation or not, the truth remains that the Holy Spirit inspired limited human beings in particular situations to write the books of the Bible. The Spirit inspired four gospels rather than just one in order to lead the Church to a better grasp of God's revelation.

The principle that the Holy Spirit guides the Church gradually to a fuller understanding of truth is relevant to our study of Mary. By exploring the books of the New Testament and examining the development of their teaching about Mary, we can discover that the Holy Spirit led the early Church to a deeper appreciation of Mary's role in our Redemption.

THE GOSPELS AND OTHER NEW TESTAMENT BOOKS RELATING TO MARY

The four gospels have for their main purpose the proclamation of Christ as Son of God and Savior of the world. They offer few details about the first thirty years of Christ's life, focusing instead on his public ministry, death, and resurrection. They speak infrequently of Mary, and when they do, their aim is to shed light on Christ and his mission. But the gospels still tell us enough about Mary to reveal her as the most important woman in the history of the human race.

Because our knowledge of Jesus Christ and his Mother is drawn largely from the gospels, we should be aware of the gospels' nature and purpose. Some people have supposed that the gospels are simple documents written by four individuals shortly after the Resurrection to retell the life and teaching of Jesus. But recent advances in Scripture scholarship have shown that the gospels are much more.

The gospels were written more than thirty years after Christ's Resurrection, and the Church recognizes three stages in their development. The first stage was the life and teaching of Jesus himself. The second was the oral preaching of early believers and written collections of Jesus' sayings and miracles. The third stage was the work of the gospel writers, the evangelists. They collected materials about Jesus and adapted them to meet the needs of specific audiences, then put them into the gospels we know today (C 126).

Thus the evangelists put the gospels into their present form from materials which had been selected, shaped, and treasured by the Church. The gospels take on a special authority because they are the witness, not just of four people, but of the Christian community.

The best evidence indicates that the first gospel, that of Mark, was written about A.D. 65-70. Matthew was composed about A.D. 80-85 and Luke was composed about A.D. 80-90; both used Mark as a source, which explains the similarities among the three. Matthew and Luke supplemented what they found in Mark with material from a collection of the sayings of Jesus, and each used other sources as well. The Gospel of John appears to have developed independently of the other three. It was written after them, about A.D. 90-95, and reflects a different set of sources and a longer period of meditation upon the meaning of Christ's life.

An important reason for differences among the gospels is that each author was writing for a specific audience and each had a special purpose in mind. They had much material available to them. John's Gospel remarks that the whole world could not contain the books which might be written about Jesus (21:25). So each one selected those parts of Christ's life and teaching which illustrated the points he wanted to emphasize. Each one gave a particular "slant" to his gospel, depending on the kind of portrait he wanted to paint of Christ and the audience he wanted to reach.

This does not mean that the evangelists were dishonest. Ask two athletes about the marathon, and one may describe the rigors of training while the other recounts the euphoria of finishing. An athlete will talk about a race in one way with runners and in another with his family. So, too, the authors of the gospels varied their approach according to their special purposes and audiences.

Mark wrote his gospel for gentile (non-Jewish) Christians faced with persecution. Mark urged his readers to be steadfast as Jesus had been. He emphasized how Christ was misunderstood and rejected. He selected and arranged his material to accentuate Christ's role as the suffering Savior.

Matthew wrote for Christians who had converted from Judaism. He showed how the Old Testament pointed to Jesus as the Messiah. He referred often to Old Testament prophecies which shed light on Christ's mission, and he selected material from Christ's life and teaching which would identify Jesus as the Savior of Israel.

Luke wrote his gospel as the first half of a two-part work which included the Acts of the Apostles. Both parts were written for non-Jewish Christians. Both have the same purpose, to show that Christ came to save all people. By the time Luke wrote, Jerusalem had been destroyed by the Romans, and it was clear that a majority of Jews had not accepted Christ. Gentile Christians were asking why. In response, Luke took a positive approach, showing that many faithful Jews had indeed accepted Christ. Christianity was *the* true religion for them and for every person on earth.

John's Gospel is the result of years of reflection on the significance of Jesus' words and deeds. The author wrote for a particular community, perhaps in Asia Minor. John proclaimed Christ as Son of God, who existed from all eternity and who now ministers to his Church through his word and sacraments.

The four gospels give us most of the information we have about Mary's life on earth, and they initiate the theological study of Mary's role in our salvation. In addition to the gospels, three other New Testament books—Galatians, Acts of the Apostles, and Revelation—have some significance in our study of Mary. We will examine, in the order in which they were written, the gospels and these other New Testament books. Our purpose is to analyze what they say about Mary and to note how the Church's understanding of Mary developed.

GALATIANS

Galatians is one of the letters of Saint Paul, composed around A.D. 54 to emphasize that salvation came from Jesus Christ, not from observance of Old Testament laws. One passage relating to Mary derives from this context. Paul wrote that Christ came to make us God's children. Christ alone had the power to do this because he was both divine and human.

> But when the fullness of time had come, God sent his Son, born of a woman, born under the law, in order to redeem those who were under the law, so that we might receive adoption as children (Galatians 4:4-5).

The expression "born of a woman" is intended to show Christ's real humanity. The Son of God is also the son of a human mother. It may seem strange that Paul says no more about Mary. However, Paul began preaching about six years after Christ's Resurrection. He traveled thousands of miles, proclaimed the gospel in many lands, and founded dozens of churches. He had time only to focus on the essential details of Christ's death and resurrection. Paul relates almost nothing about the life and miracles of Jesus, so it is not surprising that he says little about Mary. But the very fact that Paul shows Christ to be the Son of God and of a human mother intimates a great deal about Mary. She is the Mother of God's Son!

THE GOSPEL OF MARK

Mark wrote his gospel for Christians who faced misunderstanding and persecution. He chose to paint a portrait of Christ as one who was misunderstood and persecuted, thereby helping his audience to identify with Christ. The colors he used to paint such a picture were applied even to Mary.

Mary appears in the gospel with relatives of Jesus who are called his brothers and sisters. Just who these individuals were will be discussed at length in Chapter Four. Here we will only note that Catholics have always understood them to be not children of Mary (the Bible never speaks of other "children of Mary") but other relatives of Jesus, most likely cousins.

By the time the relatives of Jesus appear on the scene in Mark, Jesus has been teaching for some time. He has been grieved by misunderstanding on the part of most of his hearers and by opposition from various Jewish factions. Jesus nonetheless has made a name for himself. And the reaction from his family:

> When his family heard it, they went out to restrain him, for people were saying, "He has gone out of his mind" (Mark 3:21).

> Then his mother and his brothers came; and standing outside, they sent to him and called him. A crowd was sitting around him; and they said to him, "Your mother and your brothers and sisters are outside, asking for you." And he replied, "Who are my mother and my brothers?" And looking around at those who sat around him, he said, "Here are my mother and my brothers! Whoever

does the will of God is my brother and sister and mother" (Mark 3:31-35).

Mark clearly wanted to present the relatives of Jesus as another group of people who misunderstood him. Mark wished to state that the real family of Jesus is made up of those who do God's will. He does not name Mary in verse 21 as among those who said that Jesus was out of his mind. He merely includes her among the relatives who wanted to see Jesus. But Mark does put her "outside" with those relatives, contrasting them with the disciples "around" Jesus.

Mary is mentioned by name in another episode in the Gospel of Mark. Jesus has returned to his native place to teach in the synagogue. The reaction he gets from his hearers is misunderstanding and resentment:

> Many who heard him were astounded. They said, "Where did this man get all this? What is this wisdom that has been given to him? What deeds of power are being done by his hands! Is this not the carpenter, the son of Mary, and brother of James and Joses and Judas and Simon, and are not his sisters here with us?" And they took offense at him (Mark 6:2-3).

This passage implies that Mary was seen by her contemporaries as an ordinary person. So if the Gospel of Mark were the last word on Mary, we would have little scriptural support for devotion to her. But it is not the last word.

THE GOSPEL OF MATTHEW

The author of this gospel wrote for Christians with Jewish backgrounds. He wanted to show that Jesus was the Messiah for whom faithful Jews had long hoped. He accomplished this not only by quoting Old Testament prophecies (Matthew 1:23 and Matthew 2:6) but by subtle allusions to Old Testament personalities and events.

Matthew introduces Mary in the infancy narrative which begins his gospel (Matthew 1–2). Luke does the same (Luke

1–2). The narratives, rich in symbolism, are theological statements which convey a truth transcending history, that God became one of us in Jesus Christ. Scripture scholars debate whether the details in these narratives belong to the first, second, or third stage of gospel development. But whatever the stage, the infancy narratives are inspired by God and are proclamations of religious truth.

Matthew begins with a standard Old Testament formula, a genealogy. It is designed to show that Christ was the fulfillment of the promises God made to Abraham and David. Because Jews traced descent through the father, the genealogy leads to Joseph, "the husband of Mary, of whom Jesus was born, who is called the Messiah" (Matthew 1:16). By saying that Jesus was born of Mary but not of Joseph, Matthew hints at the virginal conception. Mary's singular role is further highlighted by the presence of four other women in the genealogy: Tamar, Rahab, Ruth, and Bathsheba. Each had a special place in the line which led to Jesus. They point to Mary as Mother of the Messiah.

Matthew describes that conception immediately after the genealogy.

Now the birth of Jesus the Messiah took place in this way. When his mother Mary had been engaged to Joseph, but before they lived together, she was found to be with child from the Holy Spirit. Her husband Joseph, being a righteous man and unwilling to expose her to public disgrace, planned to dismiss her quietly. But just when he had resolved to do this, an angel of the Lord appeared to him in a dream and said, "Joseph, son of David, do not be afraid to take Mary as your wife, for the child conceived in her is from the Holy Spirit. She will bear a son, and you are to name him Jesus, for he will save his people from their sins." All this took place to fulfill what had been spoken by the Lord through the prophet:

"Look, the virgin shall conceive and bear a son,
and they shall name him Emmanuel,"

which means "God is with us." When Joseph awoke from sleep, he did as the angel of the Lord commanded him; he took her as his wife, but had no marital relations with her until she had borne a son; and he named him Jesus (Matthew 1:18-25).

Among the Jews of this time, engagement (or betrothal) was the first stage of marriage. After a woman was thus promised to her husband, any infidelity was considered adultery, and Mary would have been subject to stoning if Joseph had denounced her publicly (Deuteronomy 22:21-23). Even a private dismissal would have exposed her to disgrace. However, Joseph believed the angel who assured him that Mary's child had been conceived miraculously, and he completed the marriage ceremony.

This inspired account in Matthew's Gospel and a parallel one in Luke have taught Christians that Christ was conceived miraculously outside the normal pattern of human sexual intercourse. The virginal conception points to the fact that Jesus Christ is uniquely the Son of God.

The word *until* in the *Revised Standard Version of the Bible* and some other translations requires explanation. *Until* in English is misleading because it suggests that Joseph *did* have relations with Mary after the birth of Jesus. But the New Testament Greek does not suggest that he did. This matter will be discussed further in Chapter Four.

Matthew 2:1 states that Jesus was born in Bethlehem of Judea during the reign of King Herod. Herod was a tyrant installed in 37 B.C. as ruler of Judea (that part of the Jewish homeland around Jerusalem) by Rome, the dominant superpower in Europe and Asia. Herod died in 4 B.C., and most scholars estimate that Jesus was born about 6 B.C. (Historians who originally tried to calculate the date of Christ's birth missed by six or seven years.) Herod foreshadows the rejection of Jesus by those Jewish leaders who would later have him crucified.

According to Matthew, wise men came from the East following a star to honor Christ with gifts. Herod learned of Jesus' birth through the wise men and tried to get information of his whereabouts. But they, warned in a dream that Herod wanted to kill the child, returned home secretly. Herod, in a rage, ordered the execution of all male boys two years old and under in the vicinity of Bethlehem. Jesus escaped because Mary and Joseph fled with him to Egypt, where they remained until Herod died. They then settled in Nazareth, a small town in the district of Galilee, north of Judea (Matthew 2:1-23).

Mary, Joseph, and Jesus lived in the village of Nazareth among relatives, neighbors, and friends. Jesus practiced the carpenter's trade he learned from Joseph. Apparently, Joseph died before Christ began his public ministry, for there is no mention of Joseph's activity after that time.

When Jesus was about the age of thirty (Luke 3:23), John the Baptist started to preach in the Judean wilderness. Jesus saw John's preaching as a sign that it was time to undertake his own ministry. He went to John for baptism, spent forty days in fasting and prayer, then began to teach throughout Judea and Galilee (Matthew 3–4).

Matthew, like Mark, says little about Mary once Jesus begins his public ministry. He follows Mark in reporting the effort by Jesus' relatives to see him (Matthew 12:49-50). However, Matthew omits the statement that Jesus' relatives intended to restrain him because they thought he was out of his mind. In so doing, he softens the negative impression created by Mark.

Matthew describes the rejection of Jesus in his hometown in substantially the same way as Mark. Matthew speaks of Jesus as "the carpenter's son" instead of "the carpenter." In his list of the "brothers" of Jesus, he changes Joses to Joseph, perhaps a variant spelling of the name (Matthew 13:54-58).

Matthew makes no further mention of Mary. But this gospel, written about ten years after Mark, by its positive picture of Mary as Mother of the Messiah and by its softening of Mark's approach to Jesus' family, shows that the early Church was moving toward a greater appreciation of Mary's role in God's plan for our salvation.

THE GOSPEL OF LUKE
AND THE ACTS OF THE APOSTLES

After a brief prologue, Luke begins his infancy narrative with the announcement of the birth of John the Baptist (Luke 1:5-25). Two elderly residents of Judea, Zechariah and his wife Elizabeth, were childless. Both were of priestly families, and while Zechariah was serving in the Temple, the angel Gabriel (see Daniel 9:20-25) appeared to him and announced that he and Elizabeth would have a child. He doubted the angel's word and was told that he would be unable to speak until the child was born. Shortly after this event, Elizabeth conceived.

Six months later

the angel Gabriel was sent by God to a town in Galilee called Nazareth, to a virgin engaged to a man whose name was Joseph, of the house of David. The virgin's name was Mary. And he came to her and said, "Greetings, favored one! The Lord is with you." But she was much perplexed by his words and pondered what sort of greeting this might be. The angel said to her, "Do not be afraid, Mary, for you have found favor with God. And now, you will conceive in your womb and bear a son, and you will name him Jesus. He will be great, and will be called the Son of the Most High, and the Lord God will give him the throne of his ancestor David. He will reign over the house of Jacob forever, and of his kingdom there will be no end." Mary said to the angel, "How can this be, since I am a virgin?" The angel said to her, "The Holy Spirit will come upon you, and the power of the Most High will over-shadow you; therefore the child to be born will be holy; he will be called Son of God. And now, your relative Eliza-beth in her old age has also conceived a son; and this is the sixth month for her who was said to be barren. For nothing will be impossible with God." Then Mary said, "Here am I, the servant of the Lord; let it be with me according to your word." Then the angel departed from her (Luke 1:26-38).

After the angel left, Mary went to visit Elizabeth and Zechariah at their home (believed to be Ain Karim, five miles west of Jerusalem and more than sixty miles south of Nazareth). Luke reports that when Mary greeted Elizabeth, the baby leaped in her womb, and Elizabeth cried out:

> "Blessed are you among women, and blessed is the fruit of your womb. And why has this happened to me, that the mother of my Lord comes to me? For as soon as I heard the sound of your greeting, the child in my womb leaped for joy. And blessed is she who believed that there would be a fulfillment of what was spoken to her by the Lord" (Luke 1:42-45).

Mary replied with a canticle of praise known as the *Magnificat*. This canticle is woven from many Old Testament passages, and it highlights a number of themes significant in Luke's Gospel. Among these are joy, God's care for the poor, and the Lord's faithfulness in fulfilling Old Testament promises. Especially important in showing Luke's estimation of Mary is her phrase, "Surely, from now on all generations will call me blessed" (1:48).

Mary remained with Elizabeth about three months, then returned home. Luke concludes the first chapter of his gospel with the story of John the Baptist's birth and with another canticle, this one sung by Zechariah.

While Mary was in the last stages of her pregnancy, she and Joseph had to go to Bethlehem to register for a census mandated by the Roman emperor. In Luke's familiar words:

> While they were there, the time came for her to deliver her child. And she gave birth to her firstborn son and wrapped him in bands of cloth, and laid him in a manger, because there was no place for them in the inn (2:6-7).

Angels announced to shepherds the birth of Mary's child. They went and "found Mary and Joseph, and the child lying in the manger" (Luke 2:16). Of special significance is Luke's remark, "Mary treasured all these words and pondered them in her heart" (2:19).

After eight days the child was circumcised according to Jewish law, and was named Jesus. Forty days after he was born, Jesus was presented at the Temple in Jerusalem to fulfill requirements of the Jewish law. There he was recognized as the Messiah by two elderly Jews, Simeon and Anna. After Simeon praised God, he said to Mary, "This child is destined for the falling and rising of many in Israel, and to be a sign that will be opposed so that the inner thoughts of many will be revealed—and a sword will pierce your own soul too" (Luke 2:34-35).

Luke next reports that Mary and Joseph took Jesus on a Passover trip to Jerusalem when Jesus was twelve years old. Jesus was accidently left behind by Mary and Joseph as they departed from Jerusalem. After searching for three days, they found him in the Temple, speaking with teachers of the Law. To their anxious questioning, Jesus responded: "Why were you searching for me? Did you not know that I must be in my Father's house?" (Luke 2:49) Luke says that Mary and Joseph did not understand what he said to them, perhaps implying that the meaning of Christ's mission could be grasped only with more prayer and reflection. Mary devoted herself to these, for Jesus went back to Nazareth with Mary and Joseph and "was obedient to them. His mother treasured all these things in her heart" (Luke 2:51).

Luke testifies to the virginal conception of Jesus as Matthew does, but he also witnesses to the Church's growing awareness of Mary's singular place in God's designs. As the humble servant of God, Mary responds obediently to God's will, and her response occasions the miraculous conception of God's Son. She is praised by the angel and by Elizabeth. She is seen by Simeon as one who must suffer along with her son. Two times Luke describes her as one who treasures the mysterious words and works of God.

As Luke begins narrating the public ministry of Jesus, he alludes to the virginal conception of Jesus by referring to him as "the son (as was thought) of Joseph" (Luke 3:23). He places the rejection at Nazareth at the beginning of Christ's Galilean ministry. When he describes the indignation of Jesus' towns-people, Luke has them ask, "Is not this Joseph's son?" (4:22), without any reference to other family members. It is as if Luke hesitates to have even the enemies of Jesus speak of Mary in a negative way.

Luke's high estimation of Mary is even more obvious when he relates the family's visit to Jesus during his public ministry:

> Then his mother and his brothers came to him, but they could not reach him because of the crowd. And he was told, "Your mother and your brothers are standing outside, wanting to see you." But he said to them, "My mother and my brothers are those who hear the word of God and do it" (8:19-21).

Luke points out that Mary and the family are unable to reach Jesus because of the crowd. When Jesus says that his mother and brothers are those who hear the word of God and act on it, anyone who has read Luke's infancy narrative will immediately recognize Mary as one who has heard God's word, reflected on it, and obeyed it. Luke thereby places Mary before believers as an ideal and a model.

Luke does the same in another incident which only he reports:

> While he [Jesus] was saying this, a woman in the crowd raised her voice and said to him, "Blessed is the womb that bore you and the breasts that nursed you!" But he said, "Blessed rather are those who hear the word of God and obey it" (11:27-28).

In this English version, it may appear that Jesus is correcting the woman who praises his Mother. However, the Greek word translated as *rather* can mean "no, instead..." or it can mean "yes, and what is more...." Even if the first interpretation is preferred, Luke is saying that Mary is to be praised more because she keeps God's word than because she is the physical mother of Jesus. But the context of Luke's Gospel points to the second interpretation. For in the infancy narrative, Elizabeth first praises Mary for her physical motherhood: "Blessed are you among women, and blessed is the fruit of your womb" (1:42). She then praises Mary as a true believer in whom God's word is accomplished: "And blessed is she who believed that there would be a fulfillment of what was spoken to her by the Lord" (1:45). Therefore, Luke praises Mary because she is Mother of the Lord *and* because she hears and observes God's word.

In the Acts of the Apostles, Luke completes his beautiful portrait of Mary by placing her in the company of those who, after Christ's Resurrection, waited for the coming of the Holy Spirit. After naming the apostles, he says: "All these were constantly devoting themselves to prayer, together with certain women, including Mary the mother of Jesus, as well as his brothers" (Acts 1:14).

Luke begins his gospel showing that Mary heard the word of God and kept it. She received the Holy Spirit, and Christ came into the world. Luke begins Acts by noting the presence of Mary with the apostles and other believers. With them she receives the Holy Spirit, and the Church goes forth into the world. She has a unique relationship to Jesus as his physical mother. She has a special place in Christ's body, the Church.

THE GOSPEL OF JOHN

There is no infancy narrative in the Gospel of John, but a prologue (John 1:1-18) declares the existence of the Word (the second Person of the Trinity) from all eternity. John affirms that "the Word was God" (1:1) and that "the Word became flesh" (1:14) in Jesus Christ. Mary's role in the Incarnation is not mentioned, but the prologue attests that Mary's child, Jesus Christ, is God. Nothing more momentous could be said of a woman!

Mary is introduced to John's readers at a wedding feast at Cana in Galilee (2:1-11). Mary calls Jesus' attention to the fact that the hosts have run out of wine. Jesus apparently refuses to intervene, but then changes six large containers of water into fine wine. This passage presents Mary as one who believes in Jesus and who intercedes for others. It has other important implications, which will be noted in Chapter Three.

John, like the authors of the other three gospels, mentions the "brothers" of Jesus. In a transition from Cana to the next event, the cleansing of the Temple, John writes: "After this he went down to Capernaum with his mother, his brothers, and his disciples; and they remained there a few days" (2:12). In another passage John states that Jesus' brothers did not believe in him (7:5). The relationship of these individuals to Jesus will be examined in Chapter Four.

John uses a number of techniques, such as irony, paradox, and misunderstanding, to develop important themes in his gospel. Two examples of this relate to Mary. After Jesus speaks of himself as the bread that came down from heaven, unbelieving listeners murmur: "Is not this Jesus, the son of Joseph, whose father and mother we know? How can he now say, 'I have come down from heaven'?" (6:42) The situation resembles a play where we, the audience, know something the actors do not. For we have read the prologue, and we want to shout to those unbelievers: "The Word is God and has become flesh! Joseph is only his foster father!" In another scene, unbelievers object that Jesus cannot be the Messiah. Their reason: "Has not the scripture said that the Messiah is descended from David and comes from Bethlehem, the village where David lived?" (7:42) Again, we want to interrupt with the news that Jesus *was* born in Bethlehem. John, by his skilled use of literary technique, makes us notice important facts about the birth of Christ and his relationship with Mary.

Mary makes a final appearance in John's Gospel at the crucifixion of Jesus (19:25-27). The other evangelists do not include Mary among those women who witnessed Christ's death, but John places her near the cross. With her is the disciple whom Jesus loved, and Jesus entrusts them to each other. On the surface, this account may appear to be an instance of a dying son looking after his mother. But John's meaning goes much deeper, as we shall see in the next chapter.

REVELATION

Revelation belongs to that category of literature called Apocalypse, popular two hundred years before and after Christ. Its purpose was to encourage persecuted believers to persevere because God would eventually prevail. Apocalyptic literature featured figurative language, symbols and numbers, visions, heavenly messengers, and picturesque descriptions of the struggle between good and evil.

The Book of Revelation was written after A.D. 90 to give reassurance to Christians during a persecution by the Roman Emperor Domitian (81–96). The section which relates to Mary (12:1-18) draws its imagery from a number of Old Testament passages and makes several complex parallels between individuals and groups. Mary becomes an image of the Church, and the "woman clothed with the sun" (12:1) seems to be both Mary and the Church. Revelation and its relevance to our study of Mary will be discussed further in the next chapter.

WHERE THE SPIRIT LEADS

In this brief summary of New Testament passages pertaining to Mary, we have seen that to appreciate Mary's place in the Scriptures we must first know how the Bible developed. Since God inspired human beings who were limited in understanding, they came only gradually to the truth, and the Scriptures trace a path showing us where the Holy Spirit leads.

When we apply these principles to a study of Mary, we see that the earlier books of the New Testament, such as Galatians and Mark, said little about her. But in the span of a few years, New Testament writers, like the authors of Matthew, Luke and Acts, John, and Revelation, portrayed her as a Mother who miraculously conceived the Son of God and gave birth to the Savior of the world. We can conclude from this that the Holy Spirit led the Church to a better appreciation of Mary and her role in our salvation.

This is evident even from a study of the texts alone. But when we look at these same texts in the framework of the whole Bible, especially of Old Testament passages used by New Testament authors, Mary's role becomes even more significant. We turn now to this framework, and we will discover that it forms a background, allowing us to see God's "Morning Star" shining ever more brightly.

Questions for Discussion and Reflection

Have you ever thought of the Bible as a record of how God has gradually led people to the truth? Does this approach help you see how one part of the Bible (Mark 3) can appear to be so negative about Mary, while other parts of the Bible (Matthew 1–2; Luke 1–2) present her in such a positive way?

Have you ever felt disturbed by reading Mark 3, or wonder why an inspired author would write so negatively about Mary? Is it possible that Mark had limitations in the way he understood Mary's role in salvation?

Do you think that Mark and Luke, from their present vantage point of eternity, now agree which of their gospels presents the best portrait of Mary?

Activities

Note the steps in the reasoning behind our understanding of what the Bible teaches about Mary: (1) The Bible is inspired by God. (2) Inspiration means that God, who is perfect, guides and helps human beings, who are imperfect, to write about God's dealings with humanity. (3) Imperfect human beings can come only gradually to the truth, and so there is a progression in the Bible toward a clearer understanding of God's truth. (4) By noting this progression, we can determine the direction in which God is leading us (for example, from doubt to certainty about the reality of eternal life). (5) In the New Testament, there is a steady development in the understanding of Mary's role in God's plan for our salvation. (6) The direction thus marked out by the Holy Spirit is a clear indication that God wants us to honor Mary and to see her as a model of those who believe.

Now try to express this reasoning in your own words.

If you are not familiar with the stories of Tamar, Rahab, Ruth, and Bathsheba, look them up in your Bible.

CHAPTER

3

MARY IN THE BIBLE— IMAGES AND THEMES

Kay was born in New York City in 1919 of Irish-Italian immigrant parents. When she was six months old, her mother brought her to a Catholic orphanage and told the Sisters that she could no longer care for her daughter. She left Kay on an examination table and disappeared.

At this time, overcrowding at orphanages in the eastern United States was so severe that it had to be relieved through the use of "orphan trains." Babies eighteen months to three years old were placed with nurses on trains, which stopped at small towns throughout the Midwest. The babies were given to couples who promised to feed and clothe them. Those taking the babies might adopt them or keep them as indentured servants.

Kay was placed on an orphan train a year after she arrived at the orphanage. She was chosen by a childless couple in Minnesota who gave her a good Catholic education and eventually adopted her. After completing college she became a teacher, and married Phil, also a teacher. They had eleven children, the large family Kay had always wanted.

Perhaps it was Kay's hunger for family ties that made her a wonderful wife and mother. Perhaps it was this same hunger that kept her close to the Church and to the Blessed Virgin Mary. She served her Church as a teacher and choir director, and she had a special affection for Mary. She enjoyed hymns and devotions in honor of Mary, and she prayed her rosary while doing housework.

Kay died when she was only fifty-four, but her love for Mary lives on in her family. Kay was, you see, the mother of Patty, whose story began this book.

Patty's family background helps to explain her own devotion to Mary. The more we know of a person's family history, the better we can understand that person. This is true of Patty, and it is certainly true of Mary, the Mother of Jesus.

THE HOUSE OF DAVID
AND THE QUEEN MOTHER

The old king lay on his deathbed. His oldest son, aware that his father had promised the throne to another, began to accumulate weapons and make alliances with the most powerful politicians and military officers in the country.

But the mother of the prince to whom the throne had been pledged went to the king and bowed down before him. She reminded him of his oath that her son should rule the kingdom. The king designated him ruler on that very day; as a result the young prince was acclaimed king by the people and the army, and support for his rival collapsed.

Soon after the new king was enthroned, his mother came to see him. The young king rose, bowed down to her as she had bowed down to his father, and provided a throne for her on his right.

The old king was David. The son who succeeded him was Solomon. The mother was Bathsheba. By paying homage to his mother and setting up a throne for her, Solomon established an institution that would endure as long as the kingdom of David, that of the "queen mother" (1 Kings 1–2).

David, Solomon, and many of the kings who succeeded them kept harems. Each wife naturally sought favors for her own children, and might be motivated by self-interest as well. The mother of the king, on the other hand, was the one through whom the king had received the throne. Her well-being was inescapably linked with his, and she could be trusted as a confidant and advisor. The queen mother became an essential part of Judah's kingship, the "house of David." Each queen mother was listed in the succession records of the kings of Judah (1 Kings 14:21; 15:13; 2 Kings 12:1; 14:2; 15:2...).

For almost four hundred years, the institution of the queen mother was a fact of life in Judah. The king succeeded to the throne through his mother. The queen mother was counselor to the king, and in at least one case ruled for a time after the son died (2 Kings 11:1-3). When the Jewish people thought of the house of David, therefore, they would picture the king on his throne, and at his right, the queen mother on her throne.

When the kings of David's line fell away from the covenant and put their trust in foreign alliances rather than in God, charismatic leaders, called prophets, would confront them. At times, the prophets foretold that the king would be replaced, and in one significant instance the prediction was made through the queen mother.

The year was about 734 B.C. Ahaz was king of Judah, and to thwart a hostile military alliance, he decided to appeal to the pagan king of Assyria. The prophet Isaiah approached Ahaz and told him to put his trust in God instead, promising that God would give him any sign he asked for. But Ahaz had long since abandoned faith in God; he hypocritically protested that he would not dare to tempt God. Isaiah rebuked the king and told him that God would give a sign anyway: "Hear then, O house of David!...The young woman is with child, and shall bear a son, and shall name him Immanuel" (Isaiah 7:13-14). By the time Immanuel was a young boy, Isaiah promised, the enemies Ahaz feared would be destroyed.

Most scholars think that the young woman was Abi, the young wife of Ahaz (2 Kings 18:2). Her son, Hezekiah, would be a sign that God was with Judah, and indeed he proved to be one of the greatest of the successors of David. So Isaiah promised that the House of David would be continued through a woman, Hezekiah's queen mother (2 Kings 18:2). This is noteworthy in that it points out the importance of the queen mother.

It becomes even more meaningful because New Testament evangelists saw a deeper import in Isaiah's promise. The Hebrew word translated as "young woman" in English could also signify "virgin." Matthew and Luke were inspired by God to regard Abi and Hezekiah as dim foreshadowings of a far greater mother and child, the Virgin Mary and her son, Jesus.

HOUSE OF DAVID
AND QUEEN MOTHER, FOREVER

Hezekiah was a good king, and many Jews no doubt hoped that he would make the kingdom what it had been under King David, a power in the Middle East. But this was not to happen. After Hezekiah, the kingdom of Judah declined until Jerusalem was destroyed by the Babylonians in 587 B.C. and most of the people were led into exile.

When Babylon was defeated by Persia, Jews were allowed to return home, but Judah remained weak and vulnerable. One nation after another kept the Jews under subjugation. To all appearances, the House of David was extinct and God's covenant with the people had been broken.

That is why the genealogy which begins Matthew's Gospel is so significant. It originates with Abraham, runs through David to the Babylonian exile, then continues on to Jesus Christ. In this way, Matthew tells his Jewish Christian audience, and the world: "Appearances are wrong! God has kept the covenant made with Abraham. The house of David survived the exile. It lives forever in the person of Jesus Christ" (1:1-17).

Matthew then describes the conception and birth of Jesus. He notes:

All this took place to fulfill what had been spoken by the Lord through the prophet:
"Look, the virgin shall conceive and bear a son,
and they shall name him Emmanuel,"
which means "God is with us" (1:22-23).

"There was more to God's promise than anyone ever realized!" declares Matthew. "Isaiah may not have understood the full meaning of what God said through him, but we do!" Matthew emphasizes this truth by citing other Old Testament prophecies. Wise men came from the East following a star (Isaiah 60:1-6; Numbers 24:17), seeking the King of the Jews (Matthew 2:2). They were told that the Messiah-king was to be born in Bethlehem, in fulfillment of a prophecy found in Micah 5:1. The wise men went to Bethlehem and there "saw the child with Mary his mother; and they knelt down and paid him homage" (Matthew 2:11).

Jews who understood this passage as Matthew intended would have first exulted in the realization that God's promises *had* been fulfilled. Then they would, in imitation of the wise men, have worshiped the true king of Judah, Jesus Christ. No doubt they, too, would have envisioned him "with Mary his mother," for as a king of the House of David, he would be expected to have his queen mother nearby.

The Gospel of Luke likewise saw Isaiah's prophecy fulfilled when the Virgin Mary conceived Jesus by the power of the Holy Spirit. As the angel announced to Mary:

> And now, you will conceive in your womb and bear a son, and you will name him Jesus. He will be great, and will be called the Son of the Most High, and the Lord God will give to him the throne of his ancestor David. He will reign over the house of Jacob forever, and of his kingdom there will be no end (1:31-32).

For Luke, as for Matthew, God's promise to Isaiah was kept through the queen mother, not just the queen mother of Hezekiah, but the Queen Mother of Jesus Christ. And since God gave Jesus "the throne of his ancestor David," we should expect that Jesus, like Solomon, would establish a throne at his right hand and seat his Mother upon it "forever."

THE QUEEN MOTHER
IN THE BOOK OF REVELATION

An awareness of the House of David and the queen mother in Jewish history can help us understand an important image in the Book of Revelation. This book presumes a familiarity with other Old and New Testament writings. Over half its verses are carefully constructed of biblical citations and references. The symbols and visions in Revelation are intended to call to mind images from the past which find their completion and perfection in Jesus Christ.

Thus Jesus Christ is "the holy one, the true one, / who has the key of David" (3:7). He is "the Lion of the tribe of Judah, the Root of David" (5:5) and "descendant of David" (22:16). Jesus is "King of kings and Lord of lords" (19:16). In these verses, Revelation proclaims that Jesus is the one who fulfills all the Old Testament prophecies foretelling a Messiah-King in the line of David.

The first descendant of David, Solomon, built a Temple in Jerusalem, in which was placed the Ark of the Covenant, a portable chest symbolizing God's presence. Unfortunately, Solomon's Temple was destroyed in 587 B.C., and the Ark disappeared.

But when Jesus Christ, the new descendant of David, appeared, he established a new temple: "Then God's temple in heaven was opened, and the ark of his covenant was seen within his temple" (Revelation 11:19). With these words, John, the author of Revelation, presents Jesus Christ as one who eternally rebuilt in heaven what Solomon so fleetingly built on earth. At this point, John introduces a woman.

A great portent appeared in heaven: a woman clothed with the sun, with the moon under her feet, and on her head a crown of twelve stars. She was pregnant and was crying out in birth pangs, in the agony of giving birth. Then another portent appeared in heaven: a great red dragon, with seven heads and ten horns, and seven diadems on his heads. His tail swept down a third of the stars of heaven and threw them to the earth. Then the dragon stood before the woman who was about to bear a child, so that he might devour her child as soon as it was born. And she gave birth to a son, a male child, who is to rule all the nations with a rod of iron. But her child was snatched away and taken to God and to his throne; and the woman fled into the wilderness, where she has a place prepared by God, so that there she can be nourished for one thousand two hundred and sixty days.

And war broke out in heaven; Michael and his angels fought against the dragon. The dragon…who is called the Devil and Satan…was thrown down to the earth, and his angels were thrown down with him.…

So when the dragon saw that he had been thrown down to the earth, he pursued the woman who had given birth to the male child. But the woman was given the two wings of the great eagle, so that she could fly from the serpent into the wilderness, to her place where she is nourished for a time, and times, and half a time. Then from his mouth the serpent poured water like a river after the woman, to sweep her away with the flood. But the earth came to the help of the woman; it opened its mouth and swallowed the river that the dragon had poured from its mouth. Then the dragon was angry with the woman, and went off to make war on the rest of her children, those who keep the commandments of God and hold the testimony of Jesus (Revelation 12:1-9,13-17).

The woman clothed with the sun is a complex symbol representing both the Church and the Mother of Jesus Christ. The sun, moon, and stars are probably drawn from Joseph's vision in Genesis 37:9-10. The dragon is identified with the serpent in Genesis 3 and is called Satan. The stars swept by the dragon from the sky represent other fallen angels. The birth pangs may refer to the same pain Luke's Gospel called a sword which would pierce Mary's soul. The pangs may also refer to the sufferings endured by the Church in times of persecution.

The woman is the Mother of Christ because her child is destined to rule "all the nations." Satan's efforts to destroy him were doomed to failure, for Christ, through his Resurrection and Ascension, was "snatched away and taken to God and to his throne."

The woman is also the Church, for her children are "those who keep the commandments of God and hold the testimony of Jesus." The phrase, "time, and times, and half a time," is a traditional apocalyptic expression for a period of tribulation. Here it symbolizes the duration of the Church's life on earth, an era of persecution and trial. In vivid imagery, John describes Satan's efforts to destroy the Church. Water represents chaos and strife; the earth stands for security. God's protection is symbolized by the wings of the eagle (Exodus 19:4), and the woman's place in the wilderness recalls God's care for the Israelites during the Exodus.

Some Scripture scholars contend that the woman stands for the Church only, not for Mary. However, there is a real person behind the other symbols in the vision: the male child is Christ and the dragon is Satan. The real person behind the mother of the male child is Mary. She is an ideal embodiment of the Church because she is Mother of Christ, who is the "firstborn within a larger family" (Romans 8:29), and because she is Mother of believers who are identified with Christ (Acts 9:5). Mary is also an expression of the reality that even while the Church is being persecuted on earth, it is already reigning in heaven.

Because the woman of Revelation 12 is Mary, we should note that the Bible identifies her as our Mother. We are her children if we "keep the commandments of God and hold the Testimony of Jesus" (Revelation 12:17).

Revelation portrays Christ, then, as a new Solomon who has built a Temple and an Ark of the Covenant in heaven. Just as Solomon enthroned his queen mother at his right, so Christ has enthroned his Queen Mother, "clothed with the sun, with the moon under her feet, and on her head a crown of twelve stars." Jews familiar with the Old Testament would have expected any king in the line of David to have a queen mother. We who are Catholic recognize Mary as the Queen Mother of the King of kings.

THE NEW EVE

Cahokia Mounds, across the Mississippi River from Saint Louis, Missouri, is the location of a prehistoric American Indian city. When I visited there, I was impressed by the engineering prowess of those who built Cahokia a thousand years ago. I was even more impressed by their scientific skills. Archaeologists have discovered log posts, seemingly placed at random, which were actually components of a precise calendar allowing the Indians to determine key dates during the changing seasons by the location of the sun.

The Gospel of John, a millennium older than Cahokia, is also carefully designed to reveal important truths. At first glance it may seem simple and unsophisticated, but a careful investigation of the gospel reveals signposts that point to other biblical books and to deeper levels of meaning.

John begins his gospel with the words, "In the beginning," just as Genesis does. Scripture commentators have noted a seven-day progression in verses 1:19 to 2:11, which indicates that John intends to parallel the Genesis creation account. Light conquers darkness in Genesis and John. The Spirit comes upon Jesus in John's Gospel, recalling how the spirit of God moved over the waters in Genesis. All these features point to the ministry of Jesus as a new creation.

A special sign of the new creation is the first miracle worked by Jesus on day seven of John's new creation week, the changing of water into wine at Cana. This seventh day of creation is also the third in another pattern of days meant to foreshadow the Resurrection, that great day of new life.

> On the third day there was a wedding in Cana of Galilee, and the mother of Jesus was there. Jesus and his disciples had also been invited to the wedding. When the wine gave out, the mother of Jesus said to him, "They have no wine." And Jesus said to her, "Woman, what concern is that to you and to me? My hour has not yet come." His mother said to the servants, "Do whatever he tells you." Now standing there were six stone water jars

for the Jewish rites of purification, each holding twenty or thirty gallons. Jesus said to them, "Fill the jars with water." And they filled them up to the brim. He said to them, "Now draw some out, and take it to the chief steward." So they took it. When the steward tasted the water that had become wine, and did not know where it came from (though the servants who had drawn the water knew), the steward called the bridegroom and said to him, "Everyone serves the good wine first, and then the inferior wine after the guests have become drunk. But you have kept the good wine until now." Jesus did this, the first of his signs, in Cana of Galilee and revealed his glory; and his disciples believed in him (John 2:1-11).

God rested on the seventh day in Genesis, and the wedding party at Cana is a time of rest until Jesus' Mother calls his attention to the fact that the hosts had run out of wine. Jesus initially seems to dismiss his Mother's implicit request: "Woman, what concern is that to you and to me? My hour has not yet come" (John 2:4), then acquiesces.

In so doing, Jesus sets out on the course leading to our Redemption. In the Gospel of John, Jesus' *hour* is his death and resurrection. Cana is "the first of his signs" which will conduct him to Calvary. Jesus' hour is also the time for him to be "glorified" (John 12:23), and at Cana Jesus first "revealed his glory."

The links John carefully establishes between Genesis, Cana, Calvary, and the empty tomb are signposts which point out, among other things, Mary's role in our salvation. In Genesis 3, the first "woman" is deceived by Satan; she becomes the occasion of her husband's disobedience and of humanity's fall from God's grace. God confronts the man and woman, but offers a promise of redemption in condemning the serpent: "I will put enmity between you and the woman, /and between your offspring and hers; / he will strike your head, / and you will strike his heel" (Genesis 3:15).

Significantly, God promises salvation through the woman of Genesis rather than through the man. *Her* offspring would be attacked by the serpent, which would strike his heel in a futile effort to destroy him. But the woman's offspring would strike the head of the serpent, a blow fatal to Satan.

At Cana Jesus addresses his Mother as "Woman," something no Jewish male would do. With this unusual expression, John seems to be alluding to the woman of Genesis. He presents Mary as the "woman" in God's new creation. She becomes the occasion of Christ's first miraculous sign as he obediently does God's will and achieves our salvation.

Mary is again addressed by Jesus as "Woman" on Calvary.

> Meanwhile, standing near the cross of Jesus were his mother, and his mother's sister, Mary the wife of Clopas, and Mary Magdalene. When Jesus saw his mother and the disciple whom he loved standing beside her, he said to his mother, "Woman, here is your son." Then he said to the disciple, "Here is your mother." And from that hour the disciple took her into his own home (John 19:25-27).

On the surface, this may appear to be an instance of a dying son looking after his mother. But because, in John's Gospel, the disciple whom Jesus loves represents all believers, and because Jesus calls Mary "Woman," John clearly invites us to look for a deeper meaning.

This use of "Woman" once again hearkens back to Genesis, especially to God's promise of redemption. On Calvary, the prophecy of Genesis 3:15 is fulfilled. The woman is Mary. Her offspring, Jesus Christ, is crucified in Satan's attack against him; the serpent can only "strike his heel," for Christ will rise again. But Christ strikes the serpent's head and deals Satan a decisive defeat by his death and resurrection.

At this moment, Jesus assigns Mary a special relationship to those he has redeemed. The first woman was called Eve because she was "mother of all living" (Genesis 3:20). Mary now becomes the new Eve because she is the Mother of all believers. If we are Christ's beloved disciples, Mary is our Mother, and Jesus wants us to take her into our own home.

In John's Gospel, then, Mary is shown as one who sees the needs of others and presents those needs to her son. She is portrayed as a believer who trusts in the power of Jesus to do even the miraculous. She, the new Eve, the woman whose offspring struck Satan's head, is given to us as our own Mother, and we are given to her as her children.

MARY, VIRGIN-DAUGHTER

In the Old Testament, the Jewish people are often seen collectively as a city—Jerusalem or Zion (an ancient name for Jerusalem). Jerusalem/Zion is in turn personified as a woman, for example, as Virgin-Daughter Zion (Isaiah 37:22; Zechariah 2:10-13).

The image of Virgin-Daughter is meant to accent the holiness to which the Jewish people were called by the covenant. When they fell away from the covenant, the prophets saw the people as unfaithful to God. Jerusalem became a prostitute who worshiped pagan idols instead of the one true God (Jeremiah 18:13). So Jeremiah urged the people to return to covenant faithfulness: "Return, O virgin Israel" (31:21).

There are some interesting parallels between a significant "Virgin-Daughter" passage in the Old Testament (Zephaniah 3:14-17), and Luke's description of the angel Gabriel's visit to Mary (Luke 1:28-33). These parallels have caused many Scripture scholars to believe that Luke consciously imitated Zephaniah in order to present Mary as the ideal personification of Virgin-Daughter Zion.

Zephaniah proclaims: "Sing aloud, O daughter Zion.... / Rejoice...O daughter Jerusalem!...The king of Israel, the LORD, is in your midst.... / Do not fear, O Zion.... / The LORD, your God, is in your midst" (3:14-17).

The angel says to Mary, "Greetings (or rejoice, the same word as "rejoice" in Zephaniah), favored one! The Lord is with you....Do not be afraid....And now, you will conceive in your womb" (Luke 1:28-31).

We have already seen that Luke portrays Mary as an ideal believer. In this Virgin-Daughter imagery, Mary is shown as a model for the new Israel, the Church. Even if Luke did not actually intend the parallelism pointed out above, we can be sure that Mary embodies all the ideals of the Virgin-Daughter motif in the Old Testament. And Luke certainly sees her as a model of faith and holiness for the whole Church.

MOTHER ZION

Another personification of the Jewish people and of Jerusalem is Mother Zion. Just as a mother gives birth to children and protects them, so Jerusalem gave birth to the Jewish people and sheltered them. The image of Mother Zion could embody the fondest hopes of the Jewish people, as in Psalm 87. It could be a sad expression of failure, as in Isaiah 50:1 and Hosea 4:2, when it reflected the people's tendency to worship pagan gods. But Mother Zion always embodied an ideal for the future: Jerusalem/Zion would bring forth the Messiah and a faithful people who would remain close to their God. The finest expression of this ideal is a passage from the Book of Isaiah (66:7-8,12-13).

Before she was in labor
   she gave birth;
before her pain came upon her
   she delivered a son....
As soon as Zion was in labor
   she delivered her children....
You shall...be carried on her arm,
   and dandled on her knees.
As a mother comforts her child,
   so will I comfort you;
you shall be comforted in Jerusalem.

This passage sees Zion as a mother who brings a son into the world. Zion also gives birth to children. At the same time, Zion personifies the tender love of God who holds people close and comforts them, just as a mother dandles (bounces on her knee) and comforts her child.

This imagery finds its perfection and completion in Mary. She brought forth a son, the Messiah long hoped for by the Jewish people. She became the Mother of many children when her son assigned to her his beloved disciple, who represents all believers. Through her caring devotion to Jesus, she has been a sign of the compassionate love God has for us.

The fact that Mary brings forth Jesus and is also the Mother of those who believe in Christ parallels the son/children imagery of Revelation 12. The woman of Revelation is both Mother of the Messiah and Mother of the children who are the Church. The Church is also an expression of God's love for people. For these reasons, there is a close relationship between Mary and the Church. Mary personifies the Church. She also stands as a model of what every member of the Church should be. In Mother Zion, Isaiah saw the Jewish community and sensed God's love. In Mother Mary, we see the Church and are embraced by the love of God.

IMAGES AND THEMES

Just as Patty's family history provides insights into her personality, so Mary's family history gives us a clearer understanding of the Mother of Jesus Christ. As a close inspection of ancient cities reveals signposts that lead to new discoveries, so a careful investigation into the Scriptures points out signposts directing us to hidden treasures of wisdom and truth.

The Queen Mother, new Eve, Virgin-Daughter Zion, and Mother Zion are images and themes which find their origin in the Old Testament. Cherished for a thousand years by the Jewish people, they were part of the family background of the New Testament authors who portrayed Mary to the Christian community. These authors recognized Mary as the fulfillment and perfection of the hopes personified in the Old Testament images. In their own writings, they placed signposts, often subtle and poetic, to guide readers to Old Testament passages that would reveal Mary as Queen Mother, new Eve, Virgin-Daughter Zion, and Mother Zion.

These images are now part of our family heritage. They help us understand the meaning of God's inspired word in the Bible. They stand as signposts directing us toward a better appreciation of our Catholic faith.

A familiarity with these images and themes will help us value the Church's doctrine about Mary, from the first writings of early Christian teachers to the most recent papal documents. These themes occur frequently in the liturgy of the Church, and an acquaintance with them will help us worship God and honor Mary more enthusiastically. As symbols they have a power to touch our hearts and souls in ways mere words cannot. They evoke powerful emotions which enrich our lives as believers and as human beings.

Thousands gather in churches annually for May crownings and are deeply moved by the hymns and ceremonies honoring Mary as Queen Mother. Mary as the new Eve, Mother of the living, offers hope to those who must conquer discouragement and be reborn through the grace of Jesus. The image of Mary as Virgin-Daughter has helped multitudes imitate her by saying yes to God as she did. Mary as Mother, holding Jesus in her arms, sheltering us with compassion, comforts and strengthens troubled souls. The more we reflect on the depth and beauty of the Bible's teaching about Mary, the more we will thank Jesus Christ for making his Mother our Mother too!

Questions for Discussion and Reflection

Knowing about Kay helps us understand Patty's love for Mary. Who are the people in your family background who help explain your devotion to Mary?

Which of the main themes described in this chapter (Queen Mother, new Eve, Virgin-Daughter Zion, Mother Zion) appeals most to you and best helps you relate to Mary? Why?

Paul compares Christ with Adam (1 Corinthians 15:20-26,45). In what ways is Christ like Adam? In what ways do they differ? In this chapter we have compared Eve and Mary. In what ways are they similar? In what ways are they different?

As we saw in Chapter Two, the genealogy in Matthew's Gospel lists four women who point to Mary. Eve foreshadowed Mary. The *Catechism of the Catholic Church* says that the mission of many Old Testament women prepared for that of Mary. It mentions Sarah, Hannah, Deborah, Ruth, Judith, and Esther (C 489). Can you briefly explain how each of these women foreshadowed Mary in some way? How does *your* life and mission pattern itself on Mary's life and mission?

Activities

Many other images and themes in the Bible have helped Catholics appreciate Mary. Read 2 Samuel 6:12-16, the account of David's bringing the Ark of the Covenant to Jerusalem. Then read Luke 1:39-45, the account of Mary's visit to Elizabeth. Compare the actions of David and John the Baptist and see if this helps explain why one of the Church's traditional titles for Mary is "Ark of the Covenant."

Review the material about Mary as Queen Mother. Then slowly and reflectively say the following prayer, Hail, Holy Queen.

Hail, Holy Queen

Hail, holy queen, mother of mercy, our life, our sweetness, and our hope. To you we cry, poor banished children of Eve; to you we send up our sighs, mourning and weeping in this valley of tears. Turn then, O most gracious advocate, your eyes of mercy toward us, and after this our exile, show unto us the blessed fruit of your womb, Jesus. O clement, O loving, O sweet virgin Mary.

Pray for us, O holy Mother of God, that we may be made worthy of the promises of Christ.

CHAPTER 4

MARY IN THE TEACHING OF THE CHURCH

I grew up in Perryville, Missouri, where our family attended Mass at the Church of the Assumption. Behind the main altar was a large painting of Mary's Assumption. Above the entrance was a stained-glass reproduction of Raphael's "The Madonna of the Chair." When we attended Mass, we were in the company of Mary, the Virgin who had brought Christ into this world, the woman who pointed to heaven as our final destiny.

Mary's importance in God's plan was taught by our church building. It is taught as well by the Catholic Church. Doctrines that proclaim Mary as Mother of God and affirm that she was conceived without sin, remained always a virgin, and was assumed into heaven are dogmas (official teachings) of our Catholic faith.

It is at this point that some Christians part company with the Catholic Church. They may argue that the Church has no authority to teach such doctrines. Or they may contend that such doctrines are not found in the Bible and cannot be part of the Christian faith. Our study of Church teaching on Mary, therefore, must be prefaced by a consideration of the Church itself and of the relationship between the Church and the Bible.

THE CHURCH, CHRIST'S BODY AND ABIDING PRESENCE

Some Christians do not accept the teaching authority of the Church because they view it as a mere human institution. But for Catholics the Church is the Body of Christ (1 Corinthians 12:27), a sacrament of Christ's abiding presence and mission on earth (C 738). It is a spiritual and physical community which finds its origin in Jesus himself.

The first generation of Christians believed that Christ intended to establish a Church. "You are Peter," Jesus said to the first among his apostles, "and on this rock I will build my church, and the gates of Hades will not prevail against it" (Matthew 16:18). He intended his Church to have leaders who would make decisions ratified by God: "Whatever you bind on earth will be bound in heaven, and whatever you loose on earth will be loosed in heaven" (Matthew 18:18). He gave these leaders authority to teach in his name when he said to his disciples, "Whoever listens to you listens to me" (Luke 10:16). He promised to send the Holy Spirit to guide the Church: "I still have many things to say to you.... When the Spirit of truth comes, he will guide you into all the truth" (John 16:12-13).

When Jesus announced that the gates of Hades would not prevail against his Church, he promised his guidance and protection until the end of time. The New Testament shows that the apostles, to whom Jesus made the promise, ordained (commissioned and consecrated) bishops like Timothy and Titus, who in turn ordained still others (Titus 1:5-9). The Catholic Church has maintained an unbroken succession of ordained bishops from the apostles to the present time. When these ministers are in union with Peter's successor, the pope, the Church believes that Christ teaches through them. Christ's promise of guidance applies to them, and we believe that Christ protects them from error when they are teaching doctrines essential to our salvation.

SACRED TRADITION

The Church's living transmission of the teachings of Christ is called sacred Tradition. Tradition, while related to Scripture, is distinct from it and is expressed in the doctrine, life, and worship of the Church (C 76–78). The Church and its teaching mission came before the Bible, for no New Testament works existed until at least twenty years after Christ's Resurrection.

Further, Church councils made the final decisions about which books should be accepted into the Bible. Without the teaching authority of the Church, without sacred Tradition, there would be no Bible, for there would have been no way to determine which books belonged in the Bible and which did not.

Tradition means "handing on," and sacred Tradition includes the way the Church has handed on the Bible. Many passages in the Bible require interpretation. The Catholic Church offers guidance to the faithful by presenting general principles of interpretation of the Bible and specific directives about particular passages. Bible passages about Mary's perpetual virginity, for example, have been officially interpreted by the Church under the guidance of the Holy Spirit. Such passages show the interaction of Scripture and Tradition within the Catholic Church, and illustrate how both Scripture and Tradition help Catholics understand God's revelation.

"THE BIBLE ALONE?"

The idea that God's truth is transmitted through Tradition as well as Scripture has always been accepted by the Catholic Church. It is rejected by those who criticize Catholics for believing "things that are not found in the Bible," and who state that we can believe "only what the Bible says."

As a priest, I have counseled Catholics who have been upset by people attacking them for believing in Mary's Immaculate Conception or in her Assumption. Some had left the Church because they did not understand the relationship between the Bible and Tradition and could not respond to such attacks. Many of these people eventually returned to the Church after making a serious study of the Church's teachings. I've often heard the remark, "If I knew then what I know now, I never would have left the Church." Our Catholic approach to the Bible and Tradition is solidly founded on the teaching of Jesus, and we should understand it clearly.

The Bible is God's inspired Word and one of God's greatest gifts to humanity. But we should not put the Bible before Christ's own Body, the Church, which under God's inspiration produced the Bible. Ask the question, "What is the pillar and bulwark of the truth?" Many Christians will answer, "The Bible, of course." But that's not what the Bible says! The Bible states that the *Church* is the "pillar and bulwark of the truth" (1 Timothy 3:15).

The Bible itself declares that all of God's truth is not found in sacred Scripture. John's Gospel closes with the statement: "But there are also many other things that Jesus did; if every one of them were written down, I suppose that the world itself could not contain the books that would be written" (21:25).

The Bible indicates that God's truth is "handed on" by preaching as well as by the written word. The New Testament reports this mandate of Paul to Timothy: "And what you have heard from me through many witnesses entrust to faithful people who will be able to teach others as well" (2 Timothy 2:2).

Scripture explicitly acknowledges traditions that have been passed on by the leaders of the Church but are not found in the Bible. Paul wrote: "…stand firm and hold fast to the traditions that you were taught by us, either by word of mouth or by our letter" (2 Thessalonians 2:15).

Finally, there is no passage in the Bible which says that the Bible is the only source of divine revelation. Therefore, anyone who asserts that the Bible is the only source of revelation is claiming something that is not in the Bible. Anyone who says we must believe only what we find in the Bible is asking us to believe something that is not in the Bible! There is far less biblical support for attacks on Catholic belief than there is for Catholic doctrines on Mary.

The Catholic Church, in its official teaching about Mary, does not ignore the Bible. We have seen in the last two chapters that the Bible says a great deal about Mary and her role in God's plan. As we continue our study, we will find that the Church builds its understanding of Mary on a solid scriptural foundation.

MODERN CHURCH TEACHING ABOUT MARY

It is impossible in a book of this size to discuss all Church teachings about Mary. Here we will focus on three significant sources: Chapter Eight of the Second Vatican Council's *Dogmatic Constitution on the Church,* Pope John Paul II's encyclical letter, *Mother of the Redeemer,* and the *Catechism of the Catholic Church.*

The Second Vatican Council set a new direction in its approach to Mary. Previous studies of Mary tended to examine her life story as an individual. Originally, the Council planned a separate document on Mary, but voted instead on October 29, 1963 to append its treatment of Mary to the document on the Church. It titled the chapter on Mary, "The Role of the Blessed Virgin Mary, Mother of God, in the Mystery of Christ and the Church." Rather than looking at Mary primarily as an individual, the Council explained Mary in the context of her relationship to Christ (and to the Father and Holy Spirit). It then examined Mary's affiliation to us in the Church.

In his encyclical letter, *Mother of the Redeemer,* Pope John Paul II followed the same pattern. His teaching on Mary is based on the doctrine of the Second Vatican Council, develops it, and explains it in detail.

The *Catechism of the Catholic Church* also follows the lead of Vatican II. Its exposition of Mary is found largely in Part One, "The Profession of Faith." Mary is first considered in terms of her relationship to Christ, to the Father, and to the Holy Spirit. "What the Catholic faith believes about Mary is based on what it believes about Christ, and what it teaches about Mary illumines in turn its faith in Christ" (C 487; see also 144, 148-149, 273, 411, 422–423, 435, 484–511, 618, 721–726). Mary is then studied in terms of her place in the Church, as "mother of the members of Christ" (C 963; see also 773, 829, 867, 964–975, 1014).

The sections cited contain most of the *Catechism*'s teaching on Mary. But she also appears in each of the other three sections. In Part Two, "The Celebration of the Christian Mystery," Mary is presented as one of those who now worship God in heaven (C 1138, 1187). Her images and statues, along with those of other saints, remind us of the "cloud of witnesses" in heaven (C 1161, 1192). The *Catechism* indicates that we are closely joined to Mary and the saints through the Eucharist and the communion of saints (C 1172, 1370, 1419, 1477).

Part Three of the *Catechism*, "Life in Christ," places Mary before believers as an exemplar of Christian holiness (C 2030). Part Four, "Christian Prayer," explains Mary's prayer for the Church, and presents her prayer as a model for our own (C 2617–2619, 2622). It invites us to pray in union with her (C 2673–2679, 2682, 2708). Her Immaculate Conception and Assumption are signs of how God answers our petition, "Deliver us from evil" (cited in C 2853).

THE CHURCH AND MARY IN THE SCRIPTURES

The three documents cited above rely heavily on Scripture. They utilize the Bible passages referred to in Chapter Two of this text to illustrate what we believe about Mary and why we believe it.

The images and themes described in Chapter Three are also used to clarify Mary's role in God's plan. For example, the *Catechism of the Catholic Church* speaks of Mary as (Virgin) Daughter of Zion (C 722), the Woman, the new Eve and Mother of the living (C 411, 726, 2618, 2853), Mother of the Church (C 963), and Queen (C 491), among other images. The *Catechism* presumes the kind of study we have already made in Chapter Three when it refers to Mary as Daughter of Zion at the Annunciation (C 722, 2619) and as the Woman at the foot of the cross (C 2618).

The Second Vatican Council in its *Dogmatic Constitution on the Church* and Pope John Paul II in *Mother of the Redeemer* likewise make frequent use of the Bible in giving their doctrine about Mary. Anyone who reads these documents will learn that the Church has employed the colors and textures of Scripture to paint its beautiful portrait of Mary.

And as we now turn to the most important doctrines about Mary, her Immaculate Conception, her role as Mother of God, her perpetual virginity, and her Assumption, we will see that there are biblical grounds for these doctrines. They are in harmony with Scripture and can be found at least implicitly in the Bible.

MARY'S IMMACULATE CONCEPTION

A glance at the headlines of a daily newspaper will show that something is seriously wrong with humanity. War, murder, crime, and evils of every description darken almost every page of the paper and of human history. A look into our own hearts reveals that something is amiss in each of us. We see the beauty of love, honesty, and mercy, but we often find it easier to hate than to love, to skirt around the truth, and to gossip rather than speak words of compassion.

The Catholic Church describes what is seriously wrong with humanity as "original sin." Following Genesis 1–3, the Church teaches that God created human beings in God's image and likeness. God gave the first humans the freedom to choose, so that they might be able to give and receive love. God invited them to do what God defined as good, and to reject what God defined as evil. Unfortunately, those first humans, named as Adam and Eve, refused to trust and obey God. Tempted by Satan, an angelic being who had rebelled against God, they decided to do what they wanted instead of what God wanted. They disobeyed God. They sinned.

Because Adam and Eve were parents of the whole of humanity, their sin affected the human nature they transmitted to their descendants. According to the *Catechism of the Catholic Church:*

> The transmission of original sin is a mystery that we cannot fully understand. But we do know by Revelation that Adam had received original holiness and justice not for himself alone, but for all human nature. By yielding to

the tempter, Adam and Eve committed a *personal sin*, but this sin affected *the human nature* that they would then transmit *in a fallen state*. It is a sin which will be transmitted by propagation to all mankind, that is, by the transmission of a human nature deprived of original holiness and justice (C 404).

The Catholic Church believes that original sin does not make us or the world wholly evil, but that it damages us in many ways. We observe its harmful effects in our own conduct and in that of others. Original sin deprives us of the union with God and the holiness granted to the first human beings, leaving us in a condition where we are subject to physical death and unable to attain eternal life. It weighs us down with the tendency to do evil instead of good, making us incapable of overcoming sin or repairing the damage caused by sin. It leaves us in a world where there is suffering and evil, where we can be hurt because people misuse freedom, where we learn bad habits from others, and where we can be a bad influence on others (C 399–409).

The New Testament brings the Good News that Jesus Christ frees us from the shackles of original sin. Romans 5 admits the existence of original sin, but recognizes as well that we are redeemed from it by Jesus Christ.

Romans 6:1-11 teaches that we gain a share in Christ's salvation through the sacrament of baptism. Baptism imparts the life of Christ's grace to abolish the death caused by sin. It erases original sin and turns us back to God. It gives us the promise of eternal life. However, we are still left with the consequences of our weakened human nature. We still have inclinations to sin and must look to Jesus for the grace to conquer sin.

The Church teaches that Mary was not touched by original sin as we are. The dogma of the Immaculate Conception proclaims that what we receive through baptism, Mary received at the first moment of her conception. She was never tainted by original sin or placed under the limits it imposes. With the help of God's grace, she remained free of all personal sin as well.

The Bible does not use the words, "Immaculate Conception," but it does show that Mary was uniquely blessed by God because she was the Mother of Jesus. Some modern Scripture scholars assert that the popular translation of Gabriel's words to Mary in Luke 1:28, "Hail, full of grace," is more accurate than recent renderings like "Greetings, favored one." The Greek *kecharitomene* implies a plenitude of grace that is both singular and permanent. This understanding that Mary was "full of grace" led early Christians to realize that Mary had been conceived without sin.

As early as the fourth century, theologians began to teach that Mary had been kept free of all sin by God because she was to be the Mother of Jesus Christ. By the seventh century, there was a liturgical observance proclaiming Mary's freedom from sin. However, there was much debate among theologians about how Mary could be free of original sin since the Bible teaches that salvation comes from Christ. In the thirteenth century, the Franciscan theologian Duns Scotus taught that Mary was preserved from all sin by the foreseen merits of Christ. God is not limited by time, and so Mary could be preserved from original sin by Christ just as those who lived and died in Old Testament times were, in the final analysis, redeemed by him.

This teaching gradually prevailed. When Pope Pius IX questioned the bishops of the world in the mid nineteenth century, he was assured that belief in Mary's Immaculate Conception was universal among Catholics. In 1854, he proclaimed the Immaculate Conception to be a dogma of the Church:

> The most Blessed Virgin Mary was, from the first moment of her conception, by a singular grace and privilege of almighty God and by virtue of the merits of Jesus Christ, Savior of the human race, preserved immune from all stain of original sin (*Ineffabilis Deus* 1854, cited in C 491).

Jesus is truly God, and is uniquely holy by reason of his divinity. Mary is human, and is holy by the grace and merits of her son. Jesus is free of original sin because he is God. Mary was kept free of original sin by the grace of Jesus. She was conceived by her parents in the normal way, but from the moment of her conception she existed in a state of union with God. She was granted the kind of grace and holiness which would have belonged to all human beings had there been no original sin.

It is also Catholic dogma that Mary remained free from personal sin throughout her life (C 493). She was not immune to the problems of living in a world touched by sin. She had to cooperate with God's grace, and she had to cope with evil, above all the unjust murder of her son on the cross. Mary was tempted as we are. But she did not sin. She cooperated with God's grace, and in this she is a model for us. When we are tempted to think that sin cannot be defeated, Mary witnesses to the fact that the grace of Christ can conquer the powers of hell.

The doctrine of the Immaculate Conception, as we have said, is not found explicitly in the Bible, but it is consistent with Bible teaching. Matthew, Luke, and John, guided by the Holy Spirit, saw Mary as the first among believers and as one specially blessed by God. The Holy Spirit led these authors to develop a direction toward a better appreciation of Mary and of her role in God's plan. The Church followed the lines of development set by the New Testament when it proclaimed the dogma of the Immaculate Conception. We can be confident, therefore, that the Church was guided by the same Holy Spirit who led the evangelists. We have every reason for believing that it is God's will that Christ's Mother be honored as Mary, conceived without sin.

MARY, MOTHER OF GOD

Catholics call Mary the "Mother of God." They do so because the New Testament clearly indicates this truth and because it follows from the reality of the Incarnation, God becoming human in Jesus Christ.

Luke's Gospel relates that God sent the angel Gabriel to Mary, a young woman of Nazareth in Galilee. Gabriel announced that Mary would have a child, the Son of God, by the power of the Holy Spirit. Mary consented, and Jesus Christ was conceived in her womb (Luke 1:26-38).

Mary then went to visit her cousin Elizabeth, who greeted

Mary as "mother of my Lord." This greeting expressed the reality that the Lord, the God of the Old Testament, was present in the womb of Mary (Luke 1:39-45). Other passages of the Bible testify to the same fact. Mary is the Mother of Jesus Christ (Matthew 1:18-25). Jesus Christ is God (John 20:28). Therefore, Mary is Mother of God.

Jesus Christ's origins are both divine and human. The miraculous conception of Jesus in the womb of Mary was the moment when the immortal, eternal God entered our history. The second Person of the Trinity (the Word), eternally joined to the one divine Nature, took on a human nature in the womb of Mary. Jesus Christ, therefore, had one divine person and two natures, divine and human. From the moment of his conception, Jesus was both God and human, and from that moment Mary has been Mother of God.

Therefore, belief in Mary as Mother of God is linked to belief in the reality of the Incarnation. This is a mystery which is beyond our understanding and must be accepted in faith. Some have refused to believe. Even in New Testament times there were those who denied that Jesus could be identified with God (John 8:12-59). Others denied that Jesus was truly human, and they would not "confess that Jesus Christ has come in the flesh" (2 John 7). Those who refused to accept either the divinity or the humanity of Christ also denied that Mary is Mother of God.

Early Church councils affirmed that Jesus is truly God and truly human. Further clarification came in the fifth century when Nestorius, the bishop of Constantinople, wrongly stated that there were two persons in Jesus Christ and that the son of Mary could not be identified with the Son of God. A general council of bishops at Ephesus in A.D. 431 condemned the teaching of Nestorius and deposed him. It affirmed that Mary is truly Mother of God because "according to the flesh" she gave birth to Jesus, who was truly God from the first moment of his conception. The expression, "according to the flesh," made it clear that Mary is not the source of Jesus' divinity. She did not give birth to God from all eternity. But since Jesus is truly God and truly human, Mary is really the Mother of God. In 451, another council at Chalcedon stated these truths as dogma, official doctrine of the Church.

When we honor Mary as Mother of God, we are actually professing our belief that Jesus is truly God. We are not saying that Mary came before God. Rather, the second Person of the Trinity, who existed from all eternity, "became flesh and lived among us" (John 1:14). The child foretold by Old Testament prophets, the child whom Elizabeth recognized as Lord, is Jesus Christ, our Lord and our God (John 20:28), and Mary is his Mother.

MARY'S PERPETUAL VIRGINITY

The New Testament, as we have seen, speaks of "brothers and sisters" of Jesus. But the Catholic Church teaches that Jesus had no blood brothers or sisters and that his Mother Mary always remained a virgin. These truths have been arrived at from the Bible and from sacred Tradition.

In biblical times, as now, "brothers and sisters" could be used in many ways. When we hear speakers address audiences as "brothers and sisters," we assume that the words refer not to blood relatives, but to friends or to members of a particular nation, group, or race. In the Old Testament, "brothers and sisters" might refer to members of the same tribe (Deuteronomy 15:12) or race (Deuteronomy 23:7), or to nephews (Genesis 13:8), cousins (Leviticus 10:4), or relatives in general (2 Kings 10:13).

The New Testament never speaks of other children of Mary or Joseph, so it is impossible to prove from the Bible that Jesus actually had blood brothers or sisters. But there are many passages which indicate that he did not.

For example, two of those who are called brothers of Jesus, namely James and Joseph (Matthew 13:56-57), are later identified as sons of a woman other than Mary, possibly Mary's sister (Matthew 27:56). And if Mary had other children, it is difficult to explain why Jesus, as he hung on the cross, would have given Mary into the care of the beloved disciple (John 19:26-27). Entrusting Mary to the beloved disciple would have made no sense if Jesus had blood brothers.

The word *brothers* is used in the New Testament for the

followers of Jesus more than one hundred times. For example, the risen Jesus asked Mary Magdalene to "go to my brothers." Mary "went and announced to the disciples, 'I have seen the Lord'" (John 20:18). Jesus said that those who do the will of his Father are his brothers (Luke 8:21).

Some people argue that Luke 2:7, referring to Jesus as Mary's "firstborn son," suggests that Mary must have had children after Jesus. But *firstborn* was a legal term for Jewish people: the firstborn was to be presented in the Temple, as Jesus was (Luke 2:22; see Exodus 13:2). Firstborn does not imply other children: An inscription dating to 5 B.C. on the grave of a Jewish woman in Egypt says that she died "giving birth to her firstborn son."

The expression in some English translations stating that Joseph "had no marital relations with her [Mary] until she had borne a son" (Matthew 1:25) also seems to point to other children. But our English word *until* implies "only up to and not beyond." The Greek and Aramaic words translated by *until* usually meant "up to" without ruling out the beyond. *Until* in English suggests that Joseph did have relations with Mary after the birth of Jesus. But *until* in the Greek or Aramaic does not suggest that he did. It focuses only on the time up to the birth of Jesus and says nothing about what happened thereafter. A similar expression in 2 Samuel 6:23 states that Michal "had no child to the day of her death." The English translation uses *to* instead of *until*, but the original word behind both phrases is the same, and obviously Michal did not have children after her death. In Matthew 28:20, Jesus says, "I am with you always, to the end of the age." (The word translated here as *to* is the same as the *until* of Matthew 1:25.) Here Jesus obviously means that he will be with us until the end of the world and beyond the end of the world, that is, forever. In the same way, Matthew 1:25 can carry the meaning that Joseph had no marital relations with Mary until and beyond the time she gave birth to Jesus.

Early Christian writers agreed that Jesus had no blood brothers and sisters and that Mary remained a virgin. Jerome (345–420) wrote that "Ignatius, Polycarp, Irenaeus, Justin Martyr, and all the other learned men going back to apostolic times" testified to the perpetual virginity of Mary. These writers had no reason for stating that Jesus was an only child except that he actually was an only child!

Our Catholic position, therefore, goes back to the earliest days of the Church and has been held for almost two thousand years. Since the Holy Spirit guides the Church, we can be sure that the Church's belief in Mary's perpetual virginity has been inspired by the Spirit.

Some people ask why Mary and Joseph would have chosen not to have other children. They witnessed the miracle of Jesus' conception and birth and realized that God had entrusted them with the greatest treasure in the history of the world, God's only Son. They understood that their task in life was to nurture and protect the Savior of the human race. Many years later, Jesus would speak of those who renounced marriage "for the sake of the kingdom of heaven" (Matthew 19:12). It cannot be surprising that Mary and Joseph would have given up their right to have other children in order to dedicate their lives exclusively to the care of God's Son.

The Church's belief in the perpetual virginity of Mary is significant because of what it says about Jesus and about us. The fact that Jesus was Mary's only child underlines his uniqueness as the only Son of God. It results in a special relationship between Mary and us. Since we are the Body of Christ (1 Corinthians 12:27), Mary is our Mother, and she has the same Mother's love for us that she has for Jesus. Jesus says to us as beloved disciples, "Here is your mother" (John 19:27).

These facts, rooted in the Bible and clarified by the Church's tradition, help us to see Christ in the clearest possible light. They help us to know Mary as the Virgin Mother of Jesus and as our Virgin Mother. These beliefs, old as the New Testament and new as today, have enriched the lives of countless generations of Catholics.

MARY'S ASSUMPTION

The Bible does not describe Mary's death or burial, and first-century records of these events have never been discovered. But very early in the history of the Church, perhaps as early as the second century, Christians began to express the belief that Mary had been taken body and soul into heaven. As early as the sixth century, perhaps sooner, liturgical feasts honoring the Assumption of Mary into heaven were observed. By the eighth century, belief in Mary's Assumption was common among Christians.

The main reason for belief among early Christians in Mary's Assumption was the fact that she was Mother of Jesus Christ. Christians found it difficult to imagine that the woman who had borne the sacred body of Jesus Christ could suffer corruption and dissolution.

John's vision in Revelation 12 of the woman clothed with the sun, with the moon under her feet, and with a crown of twelve stars provided scriptural basis for belief in Mary's Assumption. While this passage does not explicitly describe the Assumption, it provides corroborating evidence for the belief developed by the Church under the guidance of the Holy Spirit. The Bible theme of queen mother also invited Christians to realize that Jesus, King in David's line, having been enthroned in heaven, would enthrone his Mother at his right hand.

As time went on, the Assumption of Mary became for believers an accepted fact. Churches were built in honor of the Assumption of Mary. Between 1849 and 1950, over eight million Catholics, including eighty thousand priests and religious and almost three thousand bishops, petitioned the pope to proclaim the Assumption of Mary a dogma of Catholic faith.

"The whole body of the faithful...cannot err in matters of belief...when, 'from the bishops to the last of the faithful,' they manifest a universal consent in matters of faith and morals" (*Lumen Gentium* 12, cited in C 92). With this assurance, Pope Pius XII in 1950 made the following doctrinal declaration:

> Finally, the Immaculate Virgin, preserved free from all stain of original sin, when the course of her earthly life was finished, was taken up body and soul into heavenly glory, and exalted by the Lord as Queen over all things, so that she might be the more fully conformed to her

Son, the Lord of lords and conqueror of sin and death (*Lumen Gentium* 59, cited in C 966).

Pius XII did not address the question of whether Mary died before her Assumption. Most theologians today seem to be of the opinion that she died, as Jesus did. The pope did teach that by her Assumption, Mary shared bodily in the Resurrection and experienced a special union with Jesus, her son and savior.

As Pius XII indicated, the Assumption has a special relevance to us who are members of the Church. The Assumption places before us a vision of our own destiny. Through Mary's Assumption, Jesus caused her physical body to be transformed into the kind of spiritual body we will have in heaven (1 Corinthians 15:42-44). Her body, assumed into heaven, is no longer mortal, subject to the limits of space and time. It is glorified and immortal, a sign of what lies in store for all who are saved by the grace of Christ.

The Assumption may be compared with the resurrection of the body described in 1 Thessalonians 4:17, where Paul speaks of those who are alive at the end of time. They will, he says, "be caught up in the clouds together…to meet the Lord in the air; and…will be with the Lord forever." This language is symbolic and figurative, as any language must be in dealing with such a mystery, but it expresses reality. Some teachers and theologians describe Mary's Assumption in similar terms. They say that Mary has already experienced fully what we will experience at the end of time.

Seen in this way, Mary's Assumption flows naturally from her relationship with Christ and with the Church. Because Mary is Jesus' Mother, because she is the Queen Mother of the King of kings, she must have been welcomed into heaven by Jesus with splendor and celebration beyond imagining. She is in heaven now for us, her children and members of the Church, as one who directs us to Jesus and as a sign of hope that we, too, shall conquer death and "be with the Lord forever."

MOTHER, ADVOCATE, HELPER, BENEFACTRESS, AND MEDIATRIX

Throughout Christian history, Mary has been invoked under many titles. The *Catechism of the Catholic Church* uses "Mother of the Church, Advocate, Helper, Benefactress, and Mediatrix" as titles under which we invoke Mary's help (C 963, 969). These titles have not been proclaimed as dogma by the Church, but they do have a special importance by virtue of their use in the *Catechism*.

They are important also because they help explain Mary's relationship to us. Since Mary is Mother of Christ, she is Mother of us who are joined to him as members of his Body. As our Mother, Mary is an Advocate, one who supports and encourages us in our efforts to follow Christ and in our prayers to him. She is a Helper, assisting us by her own prayer and example. She is a Benefactress, a patron who invites us to receive the graces only her son can bestow. She is our Mediatrix, the one who brought Christ into the world two thousand years ago and who forever brings him to us. And as she does, she says to us, "Do whatever he tells you" (John 2:5).

The term *Mediatrix* should be understood in the context of Christ's desire that all believers should be mediators. A mediator is one who brings people together, and Christ certainly wants every believer to bring others to him as Andrew brought Peter to Jesus and as Philip brought Nathanael (John 1:40-51). We are all meant to share in the mission of Christ, coworkers with Christ in the work of salvation. When Saint Paul said, "In my flesh I am completing what is lacking in Christ's afflictions for the sake of his body, that is, the church" (Colossians 1:24), he was describing how he, and all believers, share in the redemptive work of Christ. Since all believers should be mediators and coworkers with Christ, we are surely being faithful to the Bible and to Christ when we call Mary our Mother, Advocate, Helper, Benefactress, and Mediatrix.

The *Catechism* emphasizes the fact that Mary's role in our salvation depends entirely on Christ and does not detract from him in any way. Quoting the Vatican II document, the *Constitution on the Church,* the Catechism says:

> But the Blessed Virgin's salutary influence...flows forth from the superabundance of the merits of Christ, rests on his mediation, depends entirely on it, and draws all its power from it. No creature could ever be counted along with the Incarnate Word and Redeemer; but just as the priesthood of Christ is shared in various ways both by his ministers and the faithful...so also the unique mediation of the Redeemer does not exclude but rather gives rise to a manifold cooperation which is but a sharing in this one source (*Lumen Gentium* 62, cited in C 970).

MARY AND THE CHURCH

I feel blessed to have grown up in a parish whose church building was a constant reminder of Mother Mary. All who are Catholic are blessed to be members of a Church which has followed the path marked out in the Bible and illumined by the Holy Spirit—a path leading to a greater appreciation of Mary as Mother of Christ and Mother of the Church.

Through the Church, we have learned that God's power is capable of conquering sin to such an extent that Mary could be kept free of sin by her son. We have honored Mary as Mother of God, and so have been strengthened in our belief that Jesus is our Lord and God (John 20:28). By believing in the perpetual virginity of Mary, we have been helped to see the uniqueness of Jesus as God's only Son. By proclaiming the Assumption of Mary, we have grown in our realization that the Resurrection of Christ will bring those who follow him to eternal glory. By acclaiming Mary as Mother of the Church, Advocate, Helper, Benefactress, and Mediatrix, we have been opened to the many ways Christ's grace is showered upon us and to the opportunities we have to bring Christ to others. Indeed, what Mary did at Bethlehem, she does today...and forever.

Questions for Discussion and Reflection

Catholics are sometimes criticized for believing doctrines about Mary such as those described in this chapter. But are graces like the Immaculate Conception and the Assumption beyond God's power? If we were the Son of God, would we do less for our Mother? Would there be any limit to the graces we would give her as the one within whom we would dwell? Would we not wish to bring her from her life of faith on this earth in the grandest possible manner to a life of glory in heaven?

Sometimes people ask, "Why does the Church insist on teaching the perpetual virginity of Mary? What difference does it make?" One obvious answer is that the Church believes it to be the truth! Other reasons are given in the text. What are they? Can you think of any others? Do you think that the doctrine of Mary's perpetual virginity implies that marriage and having children are not important? Why or why not?

Activities

Find a quiet place. Meditate on each of the dogmas explained in this chapter. Apply each doctrine to your own life situation, and talk to Mary about each. After considering Mary as Mother of God, ask her to bring you closer to Jesus. After reflecting on Mary's Immaculate Conception, ask her to help you avoid sin. After thinking about her perpetual virginity, ask her to help you become more dedicated to Jesus. Consider her Assumption, and pray that she will help bring you to eternal life.

Then reflect on Mary's titles as Mother, Advocate, Helper, Benefactress, and Mediatrix. Speak to her in prayer, addressing her under each of these titles.

MARY IN THE LITURGY

We human beings celebrate what we believe in. As Americans, we celebrate the Fourth of July to express our belief in the value of freedom. As we remember the events that brought our nation into being, we have an opportunity to reflect on the meaning of freedom and come to a clearer understanding of its blessings and demands.

We also celebrate those we love. For instance, birthday parties put someone we care about on center stage. They also help us grow in love for that person. Honoring an elderly parent with cake and candles shows our affection and leads us to a greater appreciation of all that parent has done for us through the years.

The Jewish people celebrated their beliefs and their love for God in many communal acts of worship. Mary and Joseph celebrated their belief in the God of Israel when they had Jesus circumcised and when they presented him at the Temple (Luke 2:21-23). They went to Jerusalem for the Passover every year (Luke 2:41).

CELEBRATING CHRIST

So it was natural for early followers of Christ to celebrate their belief in Jesus and their love for him. They ritualized their celebration in an act of worship given them by Jesus at the Last Supper, referred to as "the breaking of bread" (Acts 2:42; see Luke 22:14-20;). Each time they gathered for this celebration, they expressed their belief that Christ had died to save them, that he had risen, and that he was truly present among them. And as they listened to the Scriptures and prayed together, they grew in their appreciation of Christ and in their love for him.

The breaking of the bread (now called the Mass or the Eucharist) at first focused exclusively on Christ, the Father, and the Holy Spirit. But as time went on, as the apostles and other believers passed from this world to eternal life, it was only natural for Christians to consider their unity with them. Letters of Paul and Peter read at the Eucharist helped Christians to understand that these leaders spoke to them from heaven. Masses celebrated near the tombs of the martyrs formed a bond between them and believers on earth. Above all, Christ himself was seen as the builder of unity between those in heaven and those on earth (Ephesians 1:10).

At the Eucharist, and at other prayers of the liturgy (the official worship of the Church), Christians expressed their conviction that Christ had joined heaven to earth. In their celebrations of the liturgy, they proclaimed their love for Jesus and for the saints. They believed that the saints prayed with them and that they worshiped God with the saints. John, the author of the Book of Revelation, described this belief:

> Then I heard every creature in heaven and on earth and under the earth and in the sea, and all that is in them, singing,
> "To the one seated on the throne
>   and to the Lamb
> be blessing and honor and glory and might
> forever and ever!" (5:13)

MARY AND THE EUCHARIST

Since believers on earth and saints in heaven were joined together in worship, Christians began to consider their union with Mary, the Mother of Jesus, at the Eucharist. Precisely when this happened is still the subject of historical investigation, but the first generation of Christians saw Mary as a model of faith, prayer, and praise. Luke's Gospel presents her as the first believer in Christ, as one who meditated on God's saving actions and whose soul "magnifies the Lord" (Luke 1:46).

Scholars see evidence of Mary being honored at the Eucharist as far back as the second century. The remains of an ancient church sacred to Mary and dating to the third century have been uncovered at Nazareth. Mary was invoked in prayer as Mother of God as early as the third century, and she was honored in the Feast of the Nativity by the fourth century. By the middle of the fifth century, and possibly sooner, Mary was named in eucharistic prayers, and feasts in her honor were observed in both East and West.

In subsequent centuries, numerous feasts in honor of Our Lady were observed throughout the Church. The most significant of these proclaimed the belief of the Church about such doctrines as Mary's Immaculate Conception and Assumption. When in 1950 Pope Pius XII declared Mary's Assumption into heaven a dogma of the Catholic Church, he explained that the liturgy is a public profession of our faith and that the liturgical observance of the Assumption provided evidence of universal Catholic belief in this doctrine.

In addition to major feasts of Mary observed by the whole Church, special feasts were instituted for certain places and religious orders. Some of these feasts, such as those in honor of Our Lady of the Miraculous Medal and Our Mother of Perpetual Help, attained much popularity.

THE SECOND VATICAN COUNCIL

The Second Vatican Council, as noted in Chapter Four, emphasized Mary's relationship to Christ and to the Church. This fit in well with the Council's efforts to renew the Church's liturgy by focusing on Christ as the center of our worship and by seeing Mary as a model of faith and prayer. In its *Constitution on the Sacred Liturgy*, the Council declared:

In celebrating the annual cycle of the mysteries of Christ, Holy Church honors the Blessed Mary, Mother of God, with a special love. She is inseparably linked with the saving work of her Son. In her the Church admires and exalts the most excellent fruit of redemption and joyfully contemplates, as in a faultless image, that which she herself desires and hopes wholly to be (103: cited in C 1172).

The *Dogmatic Constitution on the Church* stated the ancient belief of the Church that through the Eucharist we are closely joined to Mary and the saints.

Celebrating the Eucharistic sacrifice, therefore, we are most closely united to the worshiping Church in heaven as we join with and venerate the memory first of all of the glorious and ever-Virgin Mary, of Blessed Joseph and the blessed apostles and martyrs, and of all the saints (50).

Because Mary is a model of true worship and because she joins us in worship as we honor her, the *Dogmatic Constitution on the Church* urged "that the cult, especially the liturgical cult, of the Blessed Virgin, be generously fostered" (67). In the years after the Second Vatican Council, the Church has followed this recommendation in many ways.

LITURGICAL YEAR MASSES IN HONOR OF MARY

In the revision of the liturgical year and in publication of new liturgical books based on the decrees of the Council, Mary has a place of special importance. The *Sacramentary* (official book of Catholic Mass prayers approved for use in the United States) lists fourteen celebrations in honor of Mary. Of these, three (Mary, Mother of God on January 1, the Assumption on August 15, and the Immaculate Conception on December 8) are solemnities, observances of the highest rank. Two (the Visitation on May 31 and the Birth of Mary on September 8) are feasts. Four (Mary's Queenship on August 22, Our Lady of the Rosary on October 7, the Presentation of Mary on November 21, and Our Lady of Guadalupe on December 12) are memorials. The remaining five (Our Lady of Lourdes on February 11, Our Lady of Mount Carmel on July 16, the Dedication of Saint Mary Major on August 5, Our Lady of Sorrows on September 15, and the Immaculate Heart of Mary on the Saturday following the Second Sunday after Pentecost) are optional.

There are six "Common" Masses in honor of Mary for use on Saturdays and other days when Masses may be chosen at the option of the celebrant. In 1980, optional votive Masses of Mary, Mother of the Church, and of the Holy Name of Mary were added in an appendix.

Mary has a place in many feasts honoring Jesus, including the Annunciation, Christmas, Epiphany, Holy Family, and Presentation of the Lord. She is an important figure in other celebrations such as those in honor of Saint Joseph and Saints Joachim and Ann, parents of Mary. Mary is mentioned or invoked in many Sunday and weekday Masses, in Masses for special occasions, and in such prayers of the *Sacramentary* as those recommended for use before and after Mass. And, as Pope John Paul II stated in his encyclical letter, *Mother of the Redeemer* (Section 3), the fact that Mary preceded the coming of Jesus is noted each year in the season of Advent.

In these celebrations throughout the liturgical year, the prayers express the Church's desire to join Mary in worshiping Christ. They ask Mary for her motherly care and protection. The readings from sacred Scripture proclaim Mary's role in God's plan to save us through her son, Jesus Christ.

In fact, Mary is a part of every celebration of the Eucharist. We ask her prayers in "Form A" of the penitential rite. In the Creed, we proclaim that Christ was "born of the Virgin Mary." In all the eucharistic prayers we remember Mary as we pray for the grace to share eternal life in her company. At every Mass we are reminded that the Christ we worship is Son of God— the second Person of the Trinity, and Son of Mary—a member of our human family.

MARY, THE LITURGY AND CHURCH DOGMA

All four great dogmas of the Church relating to Mary—her Immaculate Conception, divine motherhood, perpetual virginity, and Assumption—are celebrated in the liturgy. Three are obvious: Immaculate Conception on December 8; Mary, Mother of God on January 1; and Assumption on August 15. The liturgical observance which proclaims the Church's belief in Mary's virginity is not so easily recognized; it is the Solemnity of the Annunciation. The feast first celebrates the miraculous conception of Jesus by the power of the Holy Spirit. But the prayers and readings of the Annunciation proclaim that Jesus was conceived in the womb of the *virgin* Mary. The Annunciation is therefore an explicit statement of the Church's belief that Mary was a virgin when Christ was conceived, and an implicit reminder of the Church's teaching that Mary remained ever a virgin.

THE COLLECTION OF MASSES
OF THE BLESSED VIRGIN MARY

In 1986, a significant new liturgical collection of Masses in honor of Mary was authorized by the Catholic Church. This collection was made available in English in an interim form in 1990. In 1992, a definitive edition, the *Collection of Masses of the Blessed Virgin Mary,* was published. It consists of a special *Sacramentary* containing prayers to be used at these Masses, and of a *Lectionary* with readings from sacred Scripture.

These books have been published in a two-volume set designed for use in churches. They may be purchased (about $50 per set) at Catholic bookstores.

The *Sacramentary* of Masses in honor of Mary has a general introduction which reiterates the recommendation of the Second Vatican Council that Mary be honored in the liturgical prayer of the Church. It highlights the role of Mary as Mother of Jesus, and reminds us that Masses in honor of Mary actually celebrate God's plan to save us through Christ. Mary had an important part to play in this plan, and she still intercedes for us as Mother of the Church. When we celebrate Mass in honor of Mary, we are joined to her, our model of perfect discipleship and an image of what we are called to be. We celebrate Mass in union with Mary, and attending to this reality can enhance our ability to worship God:

Thus in union with the Blessed Virgin and in imitation of her reverent devotion, the Church celebrates the divine mysteries....The Church joins its voice to Mary's and praises God with her song of thanksgiving. The Church wishes to hear the word of God as she did and to dwell upon it. With Mary it desires to become a sharer in Christ's paschal mystery and to join in his redeeming work. In imitation of Mary at prayer in the upper room with the apostles, the Church ceaselessly implores the gift of the Holy Spirit. The Church invokes her intercession, flies to her protection, prays that she visit the faithful people and fill them with the gifts of grace, and, under her watchful and gracious gaze upon its progress, goes confidently forward with her to meet Christ (Section 13).

There are forty-six Masses in the *Collection*, arranged according to the liturgical year. There are three sets of Masses for Advent, six for Christmas, five for Lent, four for Easter, and twenty-eight for Ordinary Time. The section for Ordinary Time is subdivided into three parts. The first contains eleven Masses which honor Mary under titles derived from the Bible or her bond to the Church. The second has nine Masses honoring Mary as one who fosters the spiritual life of believers. The third consists of eight Masses celebrating Mary as an intercessor for the faithful.

Each Mass has its own entrance antiphon, opening prayer(s), prayer over the gifts, preface, Communion antiphon, and prayer after Communion. Two readings, along with a responsorial psalm and Alleluia verse, are provided for each Mass.

Most of the Masses were composed after the Second Vatican Council for individual churches and particular religious orders. They may now be used anywhere, and are recommended in a special way for shrines dedicated to Mary. They can be chosen for Saturday Masses in honor of Mary and on other days to which no special Mass is assigned.

Each Mass listed in the *Sacramentary* of Mary is preceded by an introduction, explaining the history of the Mass, its meaning, and the prayers and Scripture readings assigned to it. For example, the introduction of the Mass for "The Blessed Virgin Mary, Image and Mother of the Church," first explains how Pope Paul VI, on November 21, 1964, declared Our Lady "Mother of the Church." It indicates that this particular Mass was composed for the Holy Year of Reconciliation, 1975. It then points out the many links between Mary and the Church. Mary was joined to the Church at its beginning when she conceived Christ in her womb. When Jesus was hanging on the cross, he appointed Mary as Mother of his followers. Mary was united to the apostles in prayer as they waited for the Holy Spirit at Pentecost. In heaven, Mary cares for the Church and prays for us as we seek to follow her to eternal life.

This is only one example. There are forty-five others. Anyone studying them will receive a fine "minicourse" in those areas of liturgy, Scripture, and theology which relate to our Blessed Mother.

The formulas of the Masses, especially the prefaces, are excellent resources for personal prayer. The readings gather in one place all those Bible passages which relate to Mary, and provide rich fare for reflection and meditation. The greatest value of the *Collection of Masses of the Blessed Virgin Mary* is, of course, that they offer new possibilities for meaningful celebrations of the Eucharist to the whole Church.

THE LITURGY OF THE HOURS

The Liturgy of the Hours, also called the Divine Office, is an important part of the liturgical prayer of the Church. A pattern of Scripture-based prayer arranged for different times of the day, the Liturgy of the Hours is said or sung daily by priests, deacons, members of religious orders, and many laypeople. The Liturgy of the Hours consists of five "hours" or times for prayer: the office of readings, morning prayer, midday prayer, evening prayer, and night prayer. Each includes psalms, Scripture readings, and intercessions.

The Liturgy of the Hours follows the same calendar of feasts for the Church year as does the Mass. Therefore, the Church honors Mary in the Liturgy of the Hours on the feast days listed above. On these occasions, the readings and prayers relate to Mary and call upon her intercession. There is also a selection of "Common" readings and prayers that may be used for various occasions, and another selection which may be chosen to honor Mary on Saturdays.

A feature of the Liturgy of the Hours especially useful for prayer and reflection is the Office of Readings. The various feast days and observances in honor of Mary offer a selection of Scripture passages relating to Mary. They also include readings from Church documents and from sermons of teachers and Church leaders throughout Christian history. These readings can help us understand how the Church has viewed Mary from the first centuries after Christ down to the present day. They, too, are fine resources for prayer and meditation.

LITTLE OFFICE
OF THE BLESSED VIRGIN MARY

The *Little Office of the Blessed Virgin Mary* is a form of prayer in honor of Mary which is patterned after the Liturgy of the Hours. It originated in the ninth or tenth century and eventually became part of the Liturgy of the Hours. It was separated from the Liturgy of the Hours by Pope Pius V in 1568, but it remained popular among many priests, religious orders, and laypeople. It has been revised several times to keep it in conformity with the structure of the Liturgy of the Hours.

The Second Vatican Council, in its *Constitution on the Sacred Liturgy*, declared that any short Office which is drawn up after the pattern of the Liturgy of the Hours, duly approved, and recited by members of any Catholic religious institute in virtue of its constitutions is part of the public prayer of the Church (98). When recited in this fashion, therefore, the *Little Office of the Blessed Virgin Mary* is part of the Church's liturgical prayer.

BOOK OF BLESSINGS

The *Book of Blessings* is an official collection of blessing prayers for Catholics. It was revised by decree of the Second Vatican Council and published in the United States in 1989. There are two approved English editions. The first contains all the liturgical blessings of the Church. The second is a shorter edition that omits the blessings which are used only within a church building. This shorter edition is more suitable for laypeople, who are empowered by baptism and confirmation to pray most blessings, except those blessings for religious objects and objects used for prayer and worship. The *Book of Blessings* can be obtained at most Catholic bookstores.

The *Book of Blessings* has a special section for the "Order for the Blessing of an Image of the Blessed Virgin Mary" and another for the blessing of rosaries. Many of the other blessings refer to Mary, invoke her intercession, and have Scripture passages relating to Mary's role as Mother of Jesus and Mother of the Church. Blessing prayers, such as those for families, for married couples, for children, for expectant parents, for homes, nativity scenes, and Christmas trees, give a prominent place to Mary. And most of the blessings in the collection ask for Mary's assistance and prayers. Since these blessings are part of the liturgical prayer of the Church, they allow us as members of Christ's Body to unite ourselves to Mary as we worship God.

OTHER LITURGICAL BOOKS

Other liturgical books, such as those for Benediction, marriages, baptisms, and funerals, contain prayers which ask for Mary's intercession or refer to her as our Mother. Mary is the Mother of Jesus who is truly present in the Eucharist. She is a model of marital love and fidelity. She is the Mother of every child given new life through baptism. She is the compassionate Mother who comforts us at the death of a loved one.

MARY IN THE LITURGY

The more we attend to Mary's place in the liturgy of the Church, the more we realize how much the Church treasures Christ's words from the cross, "Here is your mother" (John 19:27). Mary's presence with us at every liturgical action helps us celebrate what we believe, for we entrust ourselves to the truths that guided her life. Mary helps us celebrate our love for Jesus, and to grow in love for him; her mother's love for Jesus surely adds warmth and devotion to ours.

Mary's presence also reminds us of the far-reaching power of the liturgy. When we attend Mass, participate in a baptism, or take part in any other liturgical prayer, we must not limit our view to what is visible. Mary's unseen but very real presence reminds us that there is much more.

As the *Catechism of the Catholic Church* explains:

The liturgy is the work of the whole Christ, head and body. Our high priest celebrates it unceasingly in the heavenly liturgy, with the holy Mother of God, the apostles, all the saints, and the multitude of those who have already entered the kingdom (C 1187).

Above all, the *Catechism* invites us to be aware of this heavenly dimension of our earthly liturgy when we take part in the Mass:

To the offering of Christ are united not only the members still here on earth, but also those already *in the glory of heaven*. In communion with and commemorating the Blessed Virgin Mary and all the saints, the Church offers the Eucharistic sacrifice. In the Eucharist the Church is as it were at the foot of the cross with Mary, united with the offering and intercession of Christ (C 1370).

During a lifetime we are called to worship God in the changing demands and moods of human life. Young and old, happy and sad, excited and weary, healthy and sick, joyful at the birth of a child and mournful at the death of a loved one—in all these circumstances of life, Mary stands with us, having experienced everything that touches us. She who once sang her *Magnificat*, she who once suffered in silence beneath the cross of her son, she who is our Mother, helps us to worship with faith, with hope, with love.

Questions for Discussion and Reflection
When you participate in the celebration of Mass, are you conscious of the presence of Mary? Do you listen to the Scriptures and

pray with the awareness that Mary and the saints in heaven are closely joined with you in adoring the Father, Son, and Holy Spirit? Do you think that attention to Mary's presence would help you worship Christ better or distract you? Why?

When you have attended baptisms, weddings, or funerals, have you ever thought of Mary as attending these ceremonies with you? Does she? Do you think that prayer to Mary for a child being baptized, a couple being married, or a person who has died might help these individuals?

People often ask, "Why does the Church celebrate the Immaculate Conception on December 8, and Jesus' birthday only seventeen days later? Shouldn't Christmas come nine months after the Immaculate Conception?" How would you answer these questions?

Activities

The next time you attend Mass, do so with an active awareness of the fact that Mary prays and worships with you. Before Mass, take a few minutes to anticipate the special presence of Christ at the Eucharist, as Mary anticipated the birth of Christ after his conception in her womb (Luke 1). Pray and listen carefully to the Scriptures, with Mary at your side, just as Mary "treasured all these words and pondered them in her heart" (Luke 2:19). Think of how often Mary must have heard the preaching of her son, and hear Mary say to you, "Do whatever he tells you" (John 2:5). At the presentation of the gifts, offer your life to God as Mary did: "Here am I, the servant of the Lord; let it be with me according to your word" (Luke 1:38). During the eucharistic prayer, stand with Mary at the cross of Christ, remembering that Jesus says to you from the cross, "Here is your mother" (John 19:27). As the time for holy Communion approaches, think of the joy Mary experienced when Jesus, risen and glorious, first appeared to her after his Resurrection. At Communion, receive Jesus with the awe and love Mary must have felt when she cradled the baby Jesus in her arms, when she welcomed him to the dinner table from his carpenter's work, when she embraced him, risen and glorious. After Communion, pray with Mary as the apostles did after the Resurrection (Acts 1:13-14). Finally, conscious that Mary and the saints in heaven have worshiped God with you, ask Mary to welcome you one day to the great liturgical celebration of heaven.

CHAPTER

6

MARY'S APPARITIONS

On February 11, 1858, three young peasant girls were looking for firewood along the Gave de Pau River near the village of Lourdes in southwestern France. Two crossed the river, leaving the third alone. This girl, whose name was Bernadette Soubirious, heard a rustling sound coming from a hillside cave known as the grotto of Massabielle. When she looked up, she saw a beautiful lady in a white dress with a blue sash. Bernadette thought she was imagining things and reached for her rosary in alarm. When the lady, who was holding a rosary, made the Sign of the Cross, Bernadette did the same. As Bernadette prayed, the lady let the beads slip through her fingers, but said nothing. When Bernadette finished her prayers, the lady vanished. Asked by her companions what she was doing, Bernadette told them that she had seen a lady dressed in white. They searched the hillside but found no one.

On February 14, Bernadette went back to the spot with some other children. A second time the lady appeared and smiled at Bernadette. Her companions saw nothing. The apparitions recurred fourteen times from February 18 to March 25, and again on April 7 and July 16. Large crowds began to gather, but only Bernadette saw the lady. In the apparitions the lady instructed Bernadette to drink from a spring which the girl discovered by scraping dirt from a damp spot near the grotto. The spring formed a stream, and the lady instructed Bernadette to have the priests build a chapel there. She told Bernadette that believers must pray and do penance for the conversion of sinners. When asked for her name, the lady said to Bernadette, "I am the Immaculate Conception."

CAN APPARITIONS BE REAL?

Was Bernadette imagining things, as she at first suspected? Could Mary, the Immaculate Conception, have appeared to a poor, unlettered peasant girl and given her the task of having a chapel built at a remote location in France? Is it possible that Mary has appeared to other human beings in the course of history?

Both the Old and New Testaments relate that God sends angels as messengers to human beings. The gospels affirm that Moses and Elijah appeared with the transfigured Christ to Peter, James, and John (Matthew 17:1-8). Therefore, it is reasonable to assume that Jesus can send his Mother as an emissary to people on earth.

In the past twenty centuries, many trustworthy and holy individuals have reported visions of Mary, often accompanied by messages that have been the source of countless blessings. One of the earliest accounts of such a vision is given by Gregory of Nyssa, a great Church leader and teacher of the fourth century. He reports an apparition of Mary to Saint Gregory the Wonderworker, another Church leader who died in A.D. 270. Since then innumerable apparitions have been reported. Many have the ring of truth about them. A number of these have taken place in the last two centuries and have been subjected to careful investigations.

WHAT DOES THE CHURCH TEACH ABOUT APPARITIONS?

The Catholic Church, basing its reasoning on the Bible and on the testimony of reliable witnesses, teaches that apparitions of heavenly beings are possible. However, the Church, distinguishing between public and private revelation, does not put apparitions on an equal footing with its basic teaching. Public revelation was completed in Jesus Christ and is found in the Bible and sacred Tradition of the Church (C 66, 78). The Bible and sacred Tradition form the "deposit of faith," the sum of those truths necessary for our salvation. Under the guidance of the Holy Spirit, these truths may be studied and more fully understood by the Church, but they can never be added to or changed.

Apparitions and visions belong to the realm of private revelation. The Church has recognized some of them as worthy of belief, but does not require that the faithful believe in them. The Church states that they do not belong to the deposit of faith. "It is not their role to improve or complete Christ's definitive Revelation, but to help [people] live more fully by it in a certain period of history" (C 67).

The Catholic Church teaches that no private revelation can claim to surpass or correct the revelation given us through Jesus Christ. Any alleged apparition which contradicts the basic teachings of the Church, therefore, cannot be accepted by the Church. As for others, the Church states that they are subject to the discernment of the faithful under the guidance of the magisterium (official leadership) of the Church (C 67).

WHAT ARE APPARITIONS?

An apparition is the appearance of a being normally invisible to human sight. Angels who have no bodies, Christ and Mary whose bodies are glorified, and saints who have "spiritual bodies" (1 Corinthians 15:44) cannot be seen with the human eye apart from some supernatural intervention caused or allowed by God. An apparition occurs when some visible representation of Christ, an angel, Mary, or a saint is seen by a human being.

We mortals cannot see Mary's body, glorified in her Assumption. However, by God's power a representation of Mary can appear which is visible to the eyes of one or more people, and words can be formed supernaturally which are audible to many (external vision). God can cause or allow a supernatural change on the retinas of a person's eyes so that a vision of Mary is perceived, or on the auditory system so that an individual hears words internally (internal vision). God can also act upon the imagination, causing images and voices like those seen and heard in dreams (imaginative vision). God can affect the intellect, so that a person perceives certain truths or realities without any particular sensible form, or in "flashes" of insight and intuition almost impossible to describe (intellectual vision). An experience where supernaturally caused words are heard but nothing is seen is called a "voice," or "locution." It may be external, internal, imaginative, or intellectual.

In whatever way an apparition takes place, it is always received by a human being who comes from a particular background, has a certain kind of education, and possesses the weaknesses and limitations common to all mortals. Every genuine apparition reported to others, therefore, is not a direct contact with Mary or Christ, but one that is conveyed through the visionary's background, education, and weaknesses. It is subject to lapses in memory, mental errors, mistaken impressions, and faulty interpretations. For this reason, experts in the realm of the supernatural, like Saint John of the Cross and Saint Teresa of Avila, have always recommended caution in dealing with information imparted through apparitions, even those known to be genuine.

COUNTERFEIT APPARITIONS

It can happen that sincere individuals think they have apparitions when they really do not. People with certain kinds of neurotic and psychotic disorders suppose that they see heavenly visitors or hear heavenly voices, when what they "see and hear" actually comes from their own disordered imaginations or minds. Some people with extremely vivid imaginations may mistakenly suppose that mental pictures they form in a natural way are supernatural visions. Some people confuse intense dreams with apparitions. All such experiences must be classified as false apparitions.

A second kind of counterfeit apparition is the fraudulent. Some people, perhaps in order to get attention, make money, or deceive others, pretend to have visions or other supernatural experiences. Recent times have provided all too many examples of deceit and fraud, of claimed visions and bogus messages from God, perpetrated by individuals who wanted fame...and donations.

A third type of counterfeit apparition is the satanic. "Even Satan disguises himself as an angel of light" (2 Corinthians 11:14). Satan can appear in much the same way as an angel can. Satan can affect the senses, imagination, and intellect of human beings who cooperate or are deceived. Many spiritual writers describe the infamous case of Magdalena of the Cross, a sixteenth-century Franciscan nun who appeared to have many spiritual gifts, including the stigmata (wounds of Christ), levitation (the ability to float above the ground), and the gift of prophesying future events. She deceived many, including some Church leaders, for decades. In danger of death, however, she confessed that she had sold her soul to Satan in return for special powers he bestowed upon her. She underwent an exorcism and apparently repented. Her story stands as a reminder of Satan's ability to deceive even the cautious.

PRINCIPLES OF DISCERNMENT

In our day, there are reports of apparitions of Mary in many places throughout the world. The Catholic Church admits the possibility of apparitions, but states that they must be submitted to a process of discernment. Since genuine apparitions are supernatural in origin, they cannot be tested in ways that satisfy scientific inquiry, which depends upon the examination of material objects. Nevertheless, long experience has given the Church a number of "tools," principles for reaching practical conclusions about whether an apparition is genuine or fraudulent, and for sorting out the mistakes and confusion which can cloud even genuine visions.

The first principle has already been given. Since all the truths necessary for salvation have been revealed by Christ and expressed in the official teaching of the Church, any purported revelation which contradicts Catholic dogma must be rejected. A "New Age" religionist has made claims of revelations from

Mary that she and Joseph have been reincarnated many times, and that both came back as nuns in the same convent in the Middle Ages! Such follies must be rejected because they contradict Catholic doctrine about death and resurrection. Even from a merely human point of view, it would be foolish to discard the Church's wisdom, resulting from twenty centuries of prayer and reflection, in favor of a disclosure claimed by a visionary.

A second principle is given by Jesus himself: "You will know them by their fruits. Are grapes gathered from thorns, or figs from thistles? In the same way, every good tree bears good fruit, but the bad tree bears bad fruit" (Matthew 7:16-17). A genuine revelation will have good effects on people. It will bring them closer to Christ and strengthen their desire to serve their neighbor. It will encourage people to grow in faith, to pray, to receive the sacraments. It will give peace of mind and heart. Several cautionary notes are in order, however. We can be sure that Satan attempts to negate genuine apparitions by leading people to wrong conclusions or otherwise sowing confusion and disorder. On the other hand, we should be aware that God is capable of bringing good out of a bad situation. The fact that people are returning to the sacraments at an alleged apparition site does not necessarily mean that the apparition is genuine. The good could be a result of God's grace working independently of the purported apparition (Romans 8:28-39).

A third principle is that genuine apparitions produce a sense of humility, simplicity, and God-centeredness. Those who have really been touched by God through an apparition of Mary or other mystical experience are humbled and awed by the greatness of God. They know how small any creature is in contrast to the Creator. They do not scold, accuse, intimidate, or threaten others. They do not claim the right to settle difficult theological disputes or to lay down guidelines in doctrinal or liturgical matters. They do not seek fame, fortune, or power, because these seem ridiculously insignificant in contrast to the God who has blessed them.

A fourth principle is that genuine apparitions will produce a willingness to submit one's judgment to that of the Church.

Those who have had a glimpse of the wisdom and knowledge of God know how frail our human intellect is, prone to mistakes and self-deception, and they are willing to seek spiritual direction. Those who have really experienced God's truth know that "the word of God is not chained" (2 Timothy 2:9), and they are not afraid to submit themselves to the judgment of the Church because they know that God's Church cannot keep God's word from having its effect.

A fifth principle is that no final judgment can be made on ostensibly genuine apparitions until they cease. It is possible for Satan to masquerade as an angel or a saint and set a trap by speaking truth for a time. Then when the visionary and others are convinced that the apparitions are genuine, Satan can spring the trap with a message designed to confuse or destroy faith. This is one of the reasons the Church does not give approval to ongoing apparitions.

A sixth principle is that any claims of an apparition should be handled with a great deal of caution. History teaches us that reports of a genuine apparition seem to trigger counterfeits among those who are mentally ill, among frauds seeking notoriety or profit, and among those who are used as tools by Satan. History also teaches us that even saints can be mistaken in the interpretation of their visions. Joan of Arc supposed, for example, that the voices which told her not to fear her martyrdom meant that she would not be put to death. Experience shows that even genuine visionaries can be mistaken when they take details of appearances, which are essentially symbolic, as fact. Any visionary's "description" of heaven, hell, or purgatory, for instance, ought to be regarded with caution since these states of being are beyond the senses. We should also be skeptical toward apparitions which supposedly relate hidden details about the life of Jesus or Mary. A number of saints have given dates for Mary's death which cannot be reconciled with one another. Even saints can confuse symbolism with fact.

LIVING CHRIST'S REVELATION MORE FULLY

In its approach to apparitions and private revelations, the Church avoids both the foolish naiveté which accepts them without careful examination and the extreme cynicism which denies their very possibility. Using the principles outlined above, the Church has given its approval to a limited number of apparitions, stating in various ways that they are worthy of belief.

The Church teaches that we do not give the assent of theological faith to apparitions. Theological faith is reserved for the truths of public revelation precisely because we are certain that God revealed them. In the case of private revelations, we give the assent of human faith: we believe them after prudent investigation because evidence indicates that they are credible.

Even when the Church gives its approval to particular apparitions, the Church does not require that we believe them. Why then should we? Because, as was stated above, they can help us follow Christ "more fully in a certain period of history." If Mary actually appears at a particular place and time, it is because she wants us to listen more attentively to what Christ has taught and done for our salvation.

The spiritual benefits flowing from approved apparitions of Mary have been immense. Entire nations have been brought closer to Jesus by Our Lady of Guadalupe. Millions have expressed their faith by wearing the miraculous medal, given by Mary in an apparition to Saint Catherine Labouré. An iron curtain and a Berlin Wall were weakened and eventually removed by the power of prayers said in response to an appearance of Mary at Fatima.

Since so much spiritual good has been realized through approved apparitions of Mary, it can be helpful to know something about those apparitions. Knowledge of them can strengthen our faith, lead us closer to God, deepen our devotion to Mary, and provide us with models for discerning newly reported apparitions.

Because the apparitions at Lourdes and the miracles which have occurred there have been so carefully documented, and because they have the widest international appeal, we shall give them special attention. A brief description of other approved apparitions will follow.

LOURDES

When Bernadette reported the apparitions of the "beautiful lady," the first response was skepticism. But after the spring emerged on February 25 at the grotto where Mary was appearing, crowds of over twenty thousand accompanied Bernadette each time she returned to the site. Miracles of healing occurred when the sick were washed in the waters of the spring. A blind man received his sight. A dying infant was cured. People began coming to Lourdes in great numbers.

Church leaders remained cautious, and civil authorities were hostile toward Bernadette and her family. The mayor of Lourdes barricaded the grotto from June to October of 1858. However, Emperor Napoleon III rescinded the order and reopened the site to visitors, reportedly after his own son was cured of a sickness by the application of Lourdes water. The crowds increased, as did the number of cures. As a result, the bishop of the diocese set up a commission to study the apparitions. After four years, the commission concluded that they had been genuine. In 1862, the bishop decreed that the faithful were justified in believing the apparitions to be certain.

In 1871, a church in honor of Mary's Immaculate Conception was dedicated at the site of the apparitions. Another church, the Rosary Basilica, with fifteen chapels, was opened in 1901. The church of Saint Pius X, with a capacity of twenty thousand, was consecrated in 1958. Hospitals, hospices, and other facilities were built to care for the hundreds of thousands of sick brought to Lourdes each year. The spring was diverted into pools where the sick could be placed into the water. Hotels and other tourist facilities sprang up to accommodate the throngs who came to Lourdes from all over the world. Millions of pilgrims visit Lourdes each year. Six million came in 1958, the centenary year.

Bernadette joined the Sisters of Charity of Christian Instruction in 1866. She was remarkable for her courage, honesty, and patience in enduring trials of sickness and misunderstanding throughout her life. She died at a convent in France in 1879 and was canonized a saint in 1933.

Many popes have spoken and written about the apparitions at Lourdes. In 1907, Pope Pius X approved a feast in honor of Our Lady of Lourdes for the entire Church. Pope Pius XII wrote an encyclical for the centenary year. Pope John Paul II has visited Lourdes.

Lourdes is renowned as a place of prayer and pilgrimage. But it is best known for its miracles. Thousands have claimed healing at Lourdes. Many of these healings have been subjected to rigorous scientific investigation, and about seventy-five have been officially declared by the Church to be miracles.

All claims of miracles at the shrine are examined by the Lourdes Medical Bureau of physicians, which includes any doctors who are on pilgrimage (generally twenty-five to one hundred). Nonbelievers are included along with Catholics and Protestants. The only cures considered are those with valid case histories, verifiable through x-rays, medical reports, and hospital records. The cures must be complete and beyond the power of medical treatment to achieve.

If the medical bureau is convinced that a particular cure is miraculous, it sends all records to the International Medical Committee of Lourdes, consisting of thirty doctors from ten countries, each doctor a recognized authority in a particular field. If this committee judges that a cure is medically inexplicable, the case is sent to the diocese of the person who has been healed. The bishop, advised by a canonical commission, conducts his own investigation. If he agrees with the findings of the doctors, he may declare that the cure is miraculous, a sign of God's special intervention.

One of the most spectacular and best documented miracles at Lourdes was that of a young Italian soldier with a cancer which had destroyed his hip and pelvic bone. Biopsies, x-rays, and hospital records confirmed the hopelessness of his condition. Near death, he was brought to Lourdes on May 27, 1963. After being placed in the spring water, he felt better and wanted to eat. Soon he was walking around his hospital room, dragging the cast which had immobilized his useless leg. X-rays and numerous examinations by doctors showed that he had grown a new hip! All doctors who studied the case agreed that no medical explanation was possible. This miracle was investigated and reported by *Reader's Digest,* April 1982, in a article, "Vittorio Micheli's Pilgrimage to Lourdes."

A fine book which carefully documents the events at Lourdes is *The Miracle of Lourdes* by Ruth Cranston, a non-Catholic journalist. Another book of special interest is *The Voyage to Lourdes,* by Doctor Alexis Carrel. A Nobel prize winner in medicine and an agnostic, Dr. Carrel became a believer when a terminally ill girl he was caring for was miraculously healed at Lourdes.

It is impossible to calculate the good accomplished at Lourdes since Mary appeared to Bernadette. Thousands have been cured of physical afflictions. Tens of millions have, like Alexis Carrel, been drawn closer to God. Skeptics who had ridiculed the miracles of the New Testament as mere fables have become believers because they have seen undeniable proof of miracles in our own day. Devout Catholics have grown in their love for Jesus and for the sacraments of the Church.

Through Mary's appearances at Lourdes, the goodness and love of God shine forth with unmistakable beauty and power. They shine forth through Mary's appearances at other approved sites as well.

GUADALUPE

The Shrine of Our Lady of Guadalupe in Mexico City, according to tradition, traces its origin back to December 9, 1531. On this day, Mary appeared to Juan Diego, a humble Indian whose people had been conquered by the Spaniards ten years before. Our Lady instructed Juan to go to the bishop, Juan de Zumárraga, and ask him to have a shrine built on the hill of Tepeyac, where Mary had appeared. The bishop treated Juan Diego with kindness, but did not believe him. When Mary repeated her request, the bishop asked Juan to have Mary give him a sign. This she did by asking Juan to fill his cloak with flowers from Tepeyac, roses which had sprung up miraculously. When Juan brought these to Zumárraga, the bishop saw an image of Mary, in Indian garb, imprinted on the cloak.

Many historians say that it is impossible to verify these details in a scientific way, but the effects of the reported apparition, the image of Mary on Juan Diego's cloak, and the shrines built on the hill of Tepeyac have affected the people of Mexico as much as anything else in their history. Widespread conversions of the Indian people followed the incident at Guadalupe, for the portrait of Mary was rich with symbolism which explained Christianity to the Indians better than words could.

Generations of believers have honored Mary by venerating the cloak of Juan Diego. The likeness of Mary is a work of art almost impossible to explain through merely natural causes. Many popes have expressed respect and veneration for the holy image and its tradition. A feast of Our Lady of Guadalupe is celebrated in many countries of the Americas on December 12. Millions of pilgrims go to Guadalupe each year, and Mary continues to strengthen the faith of believers by her presence at the shrine.

THE MIRACULOUS MEDAL

The first of the great modern apparitions of Mary took place in 1830 when she appeared to Catherine Labouré, a novice of the Daughters of Charity, at their motherhouse in Paris. In a series of visions, Mary gave Catherine instructions to have a medal struck in her honor. On one side, there was to be an image of Mary standing on a globe, surrounded by the words, "O Mary, conceived without sin, pray for us who have recourse to thee." On the other side, there were to be representations of the hearts of Jesus and Mary, with a monogram of the letter "M" surmounted by a cross and encircled by twelve stars.

Catherine brought the instructions to her confessor, Father Jean Marie Aladel. Reluctant to accept the reality of the apparitions, he finally relayed the message in 1832 to the Archbishop of Paris. The archbishop readily gave permission for the medal to be made. Fifteen hundred medals were struck and were sold almost immediately. Three Paris engravers and the French mint produced two million more medals and sold them in a few days. Soon tens of millions of the medals were being distributed in many countries. Within a short time, so many miracles were reported by those who wore the medal that it became known as the miraculous medal, a name it has retained to this day.

The apparitions were canonically approved by an archdiocesan commission in 1836, and the miraculous medal grew ever more popular. Meantime, Catherine remained hidden and unknown. She cared for old men at the convent hospital, scrubbed floors, and helped with the cooking. Only in 1876 did she reveal to her superior that she was the one who had seen the Blessed Mother. She did so in order to relay another request of Mary, that an altar and statue be placed in the convent chapel. Catherine died peacefully on December 31 of that same year. Fifty-seven years later, her body was exhumed and found to be completely incorrupt; even her eyes, which were open, were clear and blue. She was canonized in 1947, and her body lies in state in the Paris motherhouse chapel.

LA SALETTE

On September 19, 1846, two uneducated peasant children, Melanie Mathieu-Calvat, age fifteen, and Maximin Giraud, age eleven, were herding cattle on a mountain above the village of La Salette in southeastern France. They suddenly saw a vision of Mary surrounded by a globe of light. Mary, who was weeping, gave the children a message that people must repent and turn back to her son. She underscored the importance of prayer, of the Eucharist, of Lenten penance, and of preaching the gospel.

Initially, almost no one believed the two children. But a spring began to flow where they reported Mary's appearance and miraculous cures were reported. Five years later, after a canonical inquiry of the appearances and miracles, the local bishop pronounced them worthy of belief. Thousands of pilgrims began to frequent the site, and a church was erected. From this shrine began a movement of repentance and renewal that spread throughout France and Europe. Religious orders of men and women dedicated to Our Lady of La Salette were founded. The shrine is still a popular place of pilgrimage, proclaiming to the world Mary's message that all must repent and believe in the gospel.

FATIMA

On May 13, 1917, three children, Lucia dos Santos, age ten, and her two younger cousins, Francisco and Jacinta, were tending sheep in a field outside the village of Fatima in central Portugal. A flash of lightning drew their gaze to a tree, above which they saw a lady dressed in brilliant white standing on a cloud. The lady asked the children to pray for the conversion of sinners. She requested that they return to the spot on the thirteenth of each month until October.

When the children first told their story, few believed them. But as large numbers of people began to accompany them to the place of the apparitions each month, more and more people became convinced that the children were telling the truth. Local government officials, however, were hostile toward the Church and denounced the visions. On August 13, they kidnapped the children for two days, interrogating and threatening them. The lady appeared to the children on August 19 and promised that a great miracle would occur on October 13. When the day arrived, over fifty thousand people were present with Lucia, Francisco, and Jacinta. The lady told the children that she was Our Lady of the Rosary and called for prayer and penitence. Until then the day had been cloudy and wet, but suddenly the sun broke through the clouds and seemed to rotate and dance about the sky. Then the sun seemed to plunge toward the earth, causing terror among the thousands who saw the phenomenon. After several such displays, the sun finally returned to normal. This "Miracle of the Sun" was seen by nonbelievers, as well as by the devout. Journalists who had previously ridiculed the apparitions described the gyrations of the sun with a mixture of awe and respect.

Francisco and Jacinta died soon after the apparitions, as Mary had foretold. A long ecclesiastical investigation of the reported visions and revelations followed. Finally, on October 13, 1930, the local bishop declared the apparitions worthy of belief and authorized devotions to Our Lady of the Rosary at Fatima. Lucia later wrote accounts of the visions, as well as other revelations made to the children, including Mary's desire for devotion to her Immaculate Heart, the practice of receiving holy Communion on the first Saturday of each month, and several secrets she has not made public. Lucia entered the Carmelite convent at Coimbra, Portugal, in 1948.

Mary had requested of the children that a church be built where she appeared. A large shrine, the Basilica of Our Lady of Fatima, was completed in 1953. By this time, Fatima had become a place of pilgrimage, with huge crowds coming to visit the shrine and pray the rosary.

Pope Pius XII, who had been consecrated a bishop on May 13, 1917, chose Fatima for the solemn closing of the Holy Year 1950. Pope Paul VI and Pope John Paul II have visited the shrine, and Pope John Paul II noted that the message of Fatima remains valid because its content is the truth and call of the gospel itself. These three popes have consecrated the human race to the Immaculate Heart of Mary, and have repeated Mary's plea that all pray and do penance for the conversion of sinners.

An interesting feature of the Fatima revelations was Mary's call that Russia be consecrated to her and that believers pray the rosary for the conversion of Russia. The need for such a conversion became apparent only after atheistic communism gained control of Russia and its neighbors. The fall of the Soviet empire in recent years and the return of many of its people to the practice of religion may be seen as an answer to the prayers lifted up to heaven in response to Mary's request.

BEAURAING

Between November 19, 1932, and January 3, 1933, five children from nominally Catholic families reported thirty-three apparitions of Mary near a schoolyard in Beauraing, Belgium. At first, even the children were skeptical of the apparitions, but they and others were gradually convinced of their reality. Mary called for prayer and sacrifice, and for a shrine to be built as a place of pilgrimage.

The apparitions were subjected to a long Church inquiry, and in 1949 they were recognized as authentic by the bishop of the diocese. At its peak, the shrine drew several hundred thousand visitors a year. Several miracles of healing at Beauraing have been recognized as genuine. The children all married and have lived exemplary Catholic lives. They have remained constant in their loyalty to the facts of the appearances and in their devotion to Mary.

BANNEUX

Shortly after the apparitions at Beauraing ceased, an eleven year-old girl, Mariette Beco, eldest of seven children of a poor family living near Banneux, Belgium, reported that Mary had appeared to her. She experienced eight apparitions from January 15 to March 2, 1933. Mary identified herself to the girl as the "Virgin of the Poor," pointed out a spring which would be a sign of God's desire to relieve suffering, asked that a small chapel be built, and requested prayer.

The simplicity of the child, the congruity of Mary's messages with that of the gospel, and reported healings at the shrine brought large crowds to Banneux. A small chapel was blessed near the spring in 1933. The local bishop investigated the apparitions and in 1949 declared them worthy of belief.

APPARITIONS PAST AND PRESENT

Innumerable apparitions of Mary have been reported in the past twenty centuries, thousands since 1830. However, only those listed above have received ecclesiastical approval. Many so-called apparitions have been shown to be fraudulent or false, and as is evident from the accounts given above, the Church is extremely cautious in its approach to alleged apparitions.

Today reports of new apparitions abound. Catholics should be as careful and prudent as the official Church in their evaluation of these apparitions. Even where the effects of reported apparitions can be seen in tens of thousands of pilgrims who receive the sacraments and grow in their devotion to Christ, we must remember that all claimed revelations must be measured against the deposit of faith left us by Jesus Christ.

We should remember as well that even canonized visionaries had problems in remembering details of their visions. Many of them made mistakes in interpreting some aspects of what they saw or heard. Since this is true, we must be wary of putting too much faith in claimed revelations which have not been submitted to the test of time and to a thorough investigation by the Church. The principles of discernment ought to be carefully applied to any report of apparitions or revelations.

History shows that apparitions are possible, and that God works miracles. History also shows that one genuine apparition seems to stir up the weak and misguided who mistake dreams or wild imaginings for supernatural occurrences. We ought to avoid both skepticism and gullibility, advice given by Saint Paul almost two thousand years ago:

> Do not quench the Spirit. Do not despise the words of prophets, but test everything; hold fast to what is good; abstain from every form of evil (1 Thessalonians 5:19-22).

MIRACLES EVERY DAY AND EVERYWHERE

A pilgrimage to Lourdes has proven to be a great grace for millions. Many people have been encouraged to think about the supernatural and to let Jesus Christ into their hearts after they have seen evidence of miracles at other approved shrines of Mary or witnessed lesser phenomena like rosary chains turning gold in color. We know the miracles at Lourdes are real signs of God's loving care. We may suspect that golden rosaries are invitations from God to be more attentive to the gospel. But both proven miracles and unproven signs ought to call our attention to the signs and wonders that occur every day, everywhere.

There is the miracle of the Eucharist, for example, where Jesus Christ changes bread and wine into his own body and blood. There is the miracle of the sacrament of penance, where Jesus Christ, through the prayer of his minister, forgives sins and offers the new life of grace. There are the miracles of baptism, confirmation, matrimony, holy orders, and anointing of the sick. Through these miracles, Jesus Christ does today what he did two thousand years ago.

There is the miracle of prayer. As we thank Jesus Christ for sending his Mother to wake up the world from time to time, we ought to thank him also for the miracle that occurs every time we calm our restless minds and hearts and speak to his Mother. Earth is united to heaven. Mary gives us a personal audience. By her love and prayers, we are joined more closely to her son, Jesus Christ, our Lord and our God. An apparition? No. A miracle? Certainly a miracle of grace!

Questions for Discussion and Reflection

Which of the approved apparitions described in this chapter are you most familiar with? Do you personally believe they are genuine? Have approved apparitions had any effect on your attitudes toward prayer or Christian service? Why or why not?

While the kind of apparitions witnessed by Bernadette are infrequent, religious experiences wherein people feel the closeness and power of God are much more common. Can you point to a time or an event in your life when you felt the love of God or the care of Mary in a special way?

Many people claim that Mary is appearing to them today. Do you think that the Church should make a judgment on these apparitions more quickly than it does? Why?

Have you ever thought of the sacraments and of prayer as miracles? Are they?

Activities

Consider one of the claimed apparitions of Mary now going on. Carefully apply the principles of discernment to it.

The next time you attend Mass, do so with the awareness that a great miracle is taking place.

Spend a few minutes in prayer to Mary. Reflect on the miracle that occurs when the Mother of God personally listens to you and brings you closer to her son.

CHAPTER

7

MARY IN SACRAMENTALS, THE ARTS, AND LIFE

In my work as director of a Catholic correspondence study program, I receive letters from all over the United States. This one recently caught my attention:

I am a police detective. I started as a uniformed officer, and then was assigned to the narcotics squad and finally to the arson squad. I was married, but my marriage of nineteen years fell apart when my wife left for another relationship. I had not married in the Church, and now I felt mentally and physically away from the Lord.

About two years ago, I developed a longing to be close to God. I envisioned an eternity being separated from him, and it was horrifying. I thought of never seeing our Lord and his Blessed Mother. It was more than I could bear.

The longing for God began when I was sent to a fire in an abandoned house. There I observed a partially burned scapular on the floor and a Saint Joseph's Missal nearby. I felt our Lord was calling to me through his Blessed Mother. I next drove past a shrine of Our Lady, and although I had stopped there a couple of times before, I had never gone as far as the chapel. This time I did.

I attended Mass at the shrine, and I knew that our Lord was offering me an invitation to return to the Church. I accepted his invitation and came back to the faith in which I was blessed at birth. I have been wearing the brown scapular ever since. I've become active in the Church, working in Respect Life programs, trying to seek the Lord and do his will.

Mary is busy bringing people to her son, and she has many ways of touching hearts! Some people might suppose that the effect of the scapular on an arson squad detective was the result of mere coincidence. But God works through the events and circumstances of everyday life. This return of a Catholic to the faith was the product of God's grace, Mary's intervention, and the fact that parents and teachers long ago gave a little boy a love of Mary. Years later, after the boy became a man, their gift of love, Mary's intercession, and God's grace merged to bring peace and meaning back into his life.

This incident illustrates the fact that Mary *is* Mother of the Church and Mother of every human being. She reaches out to us in many ways that are not as spectacular as apparitions, but are real nonetheless. Through sacramentals, devotions, art, and literature, Mary affects our lives.

SCAPULARS AND SACRAMENTALS

A "sacramental" is a sacred sign such as a blessing or object instituted by the Church and symbolizing spiritual effects which come about primarily through the intercession of the Church. Sacramentals are not good-luck charms, objects of superstition supposedly having a power of their own. Sacramentals derive their special value from the prayer of the Church, which ultimately is a participation in the prayer of Jesus Christ.

The scapular found by the arson squad detective is one example of a sacramental. Scapulars are small squares of cloth worn around the neck to symbolize one's association with a religious community or organization. There are about twenty approved scapulars; half are related to some devotion in honor of Mary.

Of these, the brown scapular of Our Lady of Mount Carmel is the oldest and most popular. According to tradition, it was given in 1251 by Mary to Saint Simon Stock, an English Carmelite. Another commonly used scapular is the green scapular, which was shown to a Daughter of Charity, Sister Justine Bisquey-Buru, during appearances of Our Lady between 1840 and 1846. These and most other Marian scapulars have on them images of Mary and short invocations to her. As the experience of the arson squad detective shows, such symbols can have a powerful impact on people. Just as a painting or a toy that calls to mind a loved one or an event from childhood can move us deeply, so a scapular or other sacramental can call to mind Mary's love and Christ's gentle invitation to accept his grace.

MEDALS

Another sacramental of importance in Catholic devotion to Mary is the religious medal. A medal is a piece of metal or other hard substance, generally in the shape of a coin or cross, imprinted with an image or inscription and worn suspended from the neck by a cord or chain. The use of medals by Christians dates as far back as the second century. Early medals were inscribed with the name of Jesus, with images of saints, or with the cross.

The custom of wearing blessed medals blossomed in the sixteenth century, when all sorts of religious medals were used by the faithful. Especially common were medals bearing the images of Jesus and Mary.

The miraculous medal, mentioned in Chapter Six, is the most popular religious medal ever struck. It is unique in that its design came from Mary herself, who showed the medal in a vision to Saint Catherine Labouré in 1830. Tens of millions of the medals have been distributed throughout the world, and thousands of miracles and favors have been attributed to Mary by those wearing the medal. The prayer on the medal, "O Mary conceived without sin, pray for us who have recourse to thee," is an often used invocation. A novena of the miraculous medal has been approved by the Church and is prayed in thousands of parishes. There are numerous shrines in honor of Our Lady of the Miraculous Medal. In the United States, shrines are located at Philadelphia, Pennsylvania, and Perryville, Missouri.

The miraculous medal is still a powerful sign of God's love and Mary's intercession. Sister Briege McKenna, a well-known Catholic evangelist and retreat director, relates in her book, *Miracles Do Happen,* how Mary has used the miraculous medal to influence her and many others. Describing an evangelism trip to Brazil, where she ministered to the president, civil and military officials, as well as thousands of others, Sister Briege writes: "Many said, when I gave them this little medal, a token of Mary, that they felt an urge to return to the practice of their faith. Others reported physical healings and many healings of relationships" (Servant Publications, 1987, page 106).

The promise made by Mary to Saint Catherine Labouré in 1830 is still being kept today: "Those who wear this medal and who confidently say this prayer will receive great graces and will enjoy the protection of the Mother of God."

RELIGIOUS ART AND ARCHITECTURE

Most people keep pictures of relatives and loved ones. Catholics have always treasured paintings and statues of Mary, their Mother and Advocate. Early depictions of Mary, discovered in the catacombs at Rome, date back to the third century. As Christianity spread throughout the world, artists produced countless paintings and sculptures representing Mary at every phase of her life. She has been portrayed in works of art more than any other woman in history.

Great works of art in honor of Mary please our aesthetic sense and lift up our spirits to God. The *Catechism of the Catholic Church* states that the truth of our relationship with God can be expressed in the beauty of artistic works. Sacred art portrays and glorifies the transcendent mystery of God, the invisible beauty of truth and love made visible in Christ and reflected in the Virgin Mary and the saints. Genuine art draws us "to adoration, to prayer, and to the love of God, Creator and Savior, the Holy One and Sanctifier" (C 2500–2502).

Michelangelo's "Pietà" in Saint Peter's Basilica, for example, speaks volumes about God's love, the sufferings of Christ, and the sorrow Mary endured at her son's death. It has brought hope to sinners, consolation to the bereaved, and inspiration to the weary. El Greco's painting of the Annunciation invites us to meditate on the moment when "the Word became flesh." Murillo's Assumption directs our eyes toward our final destiny, eternal life in heaven. These and other masterpieces evoke "what is beyond words: the depths of the human heart, the exaltations of the soul, the mystery of God" (C 2500).

Not every image of Mary is a masterpiece, but even lesser artistic works can teach the beauty of truth. Paintings, stained glass, and statuary have opened the gospel stories about Mary to those who could not read. Little children become acquainted with Mary through figurines at the Christmas crib. Even for readers, works of art provide insights into the personality and mission of Mary which words cannot convey.

Architecture also expresses "the infinite beauty of God in works made by human hands" (*Sacrosanctum Concilium* 122, cited in C 2513). Great churches and cathedrals like Saint Mary Major in Rome, Notre Dame in Paris, and the National Shrine of the Immaculate Conception in Washington, D.C., proclaim our Catholic belief in God and our devotion to Mary in dramatic and powerful ways. I have visited each of these three churches and have been awed by their beauty, and even more by the faith of those who built them. At Saint Mary Major, I witnessed a procession of pilgrims singing familiar Marian melodies in a language I could not understand. "For sixteen hundred years," I thought, "pilgrims have been coming to this spot from all over the world to honor Mary. What a privilege to be among them!" At Notre Dame in Paris, the soaring walls of stained glass and chiseled stone summon to mind the light and love Mary brought into the world when she gave birth to Jesus. The National Shrine is a testimony of American devotion to Mary, a Mother who welcomed generations of immigrants to a new land and helped them feel at home. It is a reminder that we Catholic Americans must bring Jesus into our world as Mary once brought Jesus into hers by the power of the Holy Spirit.

These and all churches dedicated in honor of Mary gather believers together to receive Christ at celebrations of the Eucharist and the other sacraments. The blessed statues, stained-glass images, and paintings of Mary in churches are signs of Mary's divine motherhood and of her maternal care for all who follow Jesus. As the *Catechism of the Catholic Church* states, the sacred images of the holy Mother of God are related to Christ and signify Christ who is glorified in them (C 1161).

Some representations of Mary, like the painting of Our Lady of Guadalupe on the cloak of Juan Diego, have influenced the faith of millions. Another image, with a fascinating background in legend and history, is that of the Black Madonna of Czestochowa in Poland. Since the fourteenth century, this image of Mary has been a source of strength and unity to the Polish people. The election of Karol Wojtyla, Archbishop of Cracow, on October 16, 1978, as Pope John Paul II brought Czestochowa to the attention of the world, and John Paul II made a pilgrimage there in 1979.

OUR MOTHER OF PERPETUAL HELP

An image which has had a profound effect on the piety of American Catholics is that of Our Lady of Perpetual Help. It belongs to a classification of religious art known as the icon. An icon is a religious image originating among Eastern Christians and painted, generally on a wooden panel, according to definite rules to open our eyes to spiritual realities or to teach a lesson. The icon of Our Mother of Perpetual Help shows Mary holding the child Jesus in her left hand. Mary and Jesus wear fine robes and are royally crowned. Above Mary's left shoulder the angel Gabriel is portrayed holding the cross and nails of the crucifixion. Above her right shoulder is the angel Michael with a lance, spear, and vessel of vinegar and gall. Jesus is depicted as a child, in size about two or three years old, but with the facial characteristics of an older youth. He has placed both his hands in Mary's right hand, and he is looking over his left shoulder with some apprehension. In a quaint touch, Jesus' left sandal has fallen from his foot and dangles by its strap. It is as if Jesus has been looking into the future. Seeing his passion, he has rushed for comfort into Mary's arms so quickly that he has lost his sandal. Mary's face is solemn, with a touch of sadness. She gazes out at those who view the picture, as if to say, "This is my son who gives his life for you."

The original icon was painted by an unknown artist in Crete, probably in the fourteenth or fifteenth century. Near the end of the fifteenth century, a traveler stole the icon from a church in Crete and brought it to Rome. There he became mortally ill. Wishing to make restitution for his theft before he died, he asked an acquaintance to present it to a church in Rome. However, this was not done until, according to tradition, Mary herself appeared to the man's daughter, commanding that the icon be placed in the Roman church of Saint Matthew. In doing so, Mary revealed herself as Our Mother of Perpetual Help. In 1499, the icon was enshrined in the church of Saint Matthew, where it became an object of popular veneration and an occasion of many miracles attributed to Mary's intercession.

Late in the eighteenth century, leaders of the French Revolution began a violent persecution of the Church. After sacking churches and murdering many priests and religious in France, they sent an army against Rome. Pope Pius VI was captured and taken to France, where he died. The French army destroyed thirty churches in Rome, including the church of Saint Matthew. The icon of Our Lady was secretly removed from the church before it was leveled and was kept hidden for many years. Eventually, it was assigned by Pope Pius IX to the Redemptorist Religious Community, which had built a church dedicated to Saint Alphonsus Liguori where the old church of Saint Matthew had been located.

The Redemptorists enshrined the icon above the high altar of the church in 1866. They promoted devotion to Our Mother of Perpetual Help, conducting services in her honor throughout the world. These services, often in the form of weekly novena devotions, became extremely popular. In the 1940s and 1950s, thousands of churches in the United States conducted them weekly.

The favors credited to Our Mother of Perpetual Help have been countless. Most of these might not qualify as miracles in the strict sense, but to those who experience them, they are certainly answers to prayer.

Henry and Jeanne were married in 1951. About a year later, they were devastated when Jeanne suffered a miscarriage. Both worried that they might not be able to have children, but in 1954 (designated a Marian year by Pope Pius XII) Jeanne became pregnant again. Once more their obstetrician noted the kind of problems which had caused the first miscarriage. Though Jeanne was not a Catholic at the time, she and Henry sought consolation and strength at the parish church, where they started going to Tuesday night devotions in honor of Our Mother of Perpetual Help.

The devotions were a very emotional experience for them as they prayed to the Virgin Mary for help in enabling Jeanne to keep and deliver the baby. After each service Jeanne became more confident that things were going better spiritually, as well as physically. Soon the doctor began giving better reports, always with the warning that "something could go wrong." On the evening of December 7, after Vespers of the Feast of the Immaculate Conception, Jeanne gave birth to a healthy baby girl. Of course, she was named Mary!

Guy and Millie, with just a touch of humor, attribute their long and happy marriage to Our Mother of Perpetual Help. In the late 1940s, services in honor of Our Mother of Perpetual Help at the Redemptorist "Rock" church on South Grand in Saint Louis, Missouri, drew huge crowds. On Tuesday evenings Millie and a friend would leave work and go bowling, after which Millie would meet her parents for devotions at the Rock church. Her special intention was that Mary would help her find "a good Catholic husband." One evening she had some extra time before church and returned to the bowling alley. There she noticed a tall young man with an infectious smile whom she had known at school. One thing led to another, and soon she and Guy were attending the devotions together, Millie with the firm conviction that the answer to her prayers was in the pew beside her. After a lengthy courtship, Guy and Millie were married. Now, as they approach their golden wedding anniversary, they still thank Mary for bringing them together.

Such stories could be multiplied by the thousands. They demonstrate how God uses the good things of creation as vehicles of grace. A religious icon, Our Mother of Perpetual Help, has become the focal point for community prayer and devotion. Believers, gathered together as members of Christ's Body, turn to their Mother for assistance, and their lives are profoundly changed by Mary's love and God's grace.

MARY IN SONG

The city of Los Angeles, in conjunction with the World Soccer Championship held in the United States in 1994, sponsored a concert entitled *Three Tenors*. Because of the celebrity status of the tenors—Carreras, Domingo, and Pavarotti—the concert played to a packed stadium and was witnessed on television by tens of millions throughout the world. As part of the concert, Luciano Pavarotti sang Franz Schubert's "Ave Maria." As soon as the song was announced, applause filled the stadium, a testimony to the popularity of this beautiful hymn to Mary.

Music, like art, has the power to touch us deeply. The *Catechism of the Catholic Church* praises the musical tradition of the Church as "a treasure of inestimable worth" (*Sacrosanctum Concilium* 112, cited in C 1156), and quotes Saint Augustine's prayer to God in his *Confessions*:

How I wept, deeply moved by your hymns, songs, and the voices that echoed through your Church! What emotion I experienced in them! Those sounds flowed into my ears, distilling the truth in my heart. A feeling of devotion surged within me, and tears streamed down my face—tears that did me good (cited in C 1157).

Hymns in honor of Mary are a part of the musical tradition of the Church. The most ancient is Mary's own hymn, the *"Magnificat."* Many others, like the *"Ave Maria,"* have been sung for centuries. A number of Marian hymns are used in the liturgical prayer of the Church and are frequently sung in English translations. These include the *"Salve Regina," "Regina*

Coeli," *"Alma Redemptoris Mater,"* *"Ave Regina Coelorum,"* and *"Stabat Mater."* The best known are, in their English translations, the "Hail, Holy Queen" (*"Salve Regina"*) and the "At the Cross Her Station Keeping" (*"Stabat Mater"*).

Other popular Marian hymns with origins in the liturgical prayer of the Church include the *"Ave Maris Stella"* and *"O Sanctissima."* Countless other hymns were developed from other sources. "Immaculate Mary," for instance, has been sung in many languages during processions at Lourdes, and has spread from there throughout the world.

Hymns like "Mother Dear, Oh Pray for Me" and "Mother Dearest, Mother Fairest" once had enormous popularity because they were sung at devotions honoring Our Mother of Perpetual Help, novenas of Our Lady of the Miraculous Medal, and other services. Such hymns were used less frequently in the years after the Second Vatican Council, but like other music of the forties and fifties, they seem to be regaining some of their popularity. At issue is the question of whether or not they are too "sentimental." The Second Vatican Council said that true devotion does not consist in fruitless and passing emotions. But it also stated that the Church has endorsed many forms of piety toward the Mother of God and advised that we avoid "the falsity of exaggeration on the one hand, and the excess of narrow-mindedness on the other" (*Dogmatic Constitution on the Church* 67; see 66). The extremes to be avoided are maudlin sentimentality and snobbish elitism. Within these boundaries there is room for many kinds of Marian music in the Church—for the "old hymns" as well as for more recent compositions—and Vatican Council II invites us to keep an open mind toward the musical tastes and sensitivities of others.

MARY IN PRAYER

Many prayers, some of great literary and artistic merit, have been composed to honor and call upon Mary. The most ancient prayer invoking Mary's help is the *Sub Tuum Praesidium,* which dates back to the third century. It expresses the belief of the early Church that Mary is Mother of God and our Intercessor. A common English translation reads:

We fly to thy protection, O holy Mother of God. Despise not our petitions in our necessities, but deliver us from all danger, O ever glorious and blessed Virgin.

Many of the songs in honor of Mary, like the *"Magnificat,"* "Hail Mary," *"Regina Coeli,"* and "Hail, Holy Queen," are recited as prayers. The Hail Mary is the most familiar of all Marian prayers. The first part comes from the Gospel of Luke (1:28,42) and was used in the liturgy before the fifth century; the second part developed some time before the fifteenth century. It is used in the Angelus and the rosary. The Angelus, a prayer traditionally said morning, noon, and evening, is taken largely from Scripture. It developed over time, finally attaining its present form in the sixteenth century. (The rosary will be explained at length in Chapters Ten, Eleven, and Twelve.) The Memorare ("Remember, O Most Gracious Virgin Mary") is a popular prayer dating back to the fifteenth century. The Queen of Heaven is a prayer to Mary which originated in the twelfth century. It replaces the Angelus during the Easter season.

Litanies are patterns of prayer consisting of a series of invocations of praise and supplication followed by responses. The Litany of Loreto was approved by Pope Sixtus V in the sixteenth century, but it may go back to the twelfth century. It was apparently modeled on the Litany of the Saints. A new litany in honor of Mary's Queenship was promulgated in 1981 in the Church's "Rite for Crowning an Image of the Blessed Virgin Mary." Its invocations come from the Bible, from the Litany of Loreto, and from documents of the Second Vatican Council.

Various novenas in honor of Mary have been approved by the Church. The word *novena* comes from the Latin word for "nine." It refers to the custom of saying the same prayers on nine consecutive days or on the same day for nine consecutive weeks. This practice has a scriptural basis in the fact that the apostles and other believers, including Mary, waited and prayed together for nine days for the coming of the Holy Spirit at Pentecost (Acts 1–2). Novena devotions are not as popular as they were before the Second Vatican Council, but many parishes and shrines still schedule novenas, like those of the miraculous medal, in honor of Mary.

Prayer and devotions calling upon Mary provide an opportunity for us to meet Mary, to meditate on her presence and protection, and to ask for her assistance. In their more ancient forms, they remind us of the generations who have gone before us, encouraged by their love of Mary and by her solicitude for them.

MARY IN LITERATURE: THE APOCRYPHA

Ask a group of knowledgeable Catholic friends for the names of Mary's parents, and someone will answer, "Joachim and Ann." Ask what event is celebrated by the Feast of Mary's Presentation, and another will reply, "The occasion when Joachim and Ann brought Mary to the Temple in Jerusalem and dedicated her in a special way to God." Then inquire about the original source of this information. You'll likely get silence and puzzled looks.

Your Catholic friends can give you the first two answers because there is a liturgical feast honoring Mary's parents on July 26 and another commemorating her Presentation in the Temple on November 21. But unless they are *very* knowledgeable, they won't know that the source of this information is a second-century book called by scholars the *Protevangelium of James.* It belongs to a body of writings known as the apocrypha and is one of the first literary works written about Mary after the New Testament.

Apocrypha means "hidden" or "secret." The term originally applied to books "hidden" in the sense that they were intended only for readers with the ability to understand them. It now applies to all those writings which have some similarity to books of the Bible, but which were not accepted as inspired Scripture by the Church. Some of the books, like the *Letter of Barnabas,* became a respected part of Church literature, and portions of them are still used in the Liturgy of the Hours. Others were heretical, originating from groups like the Gnostics who promoted false doctrines. Still others, like the *Protevangelium of James,* were a mixture of authentic traditions, legend, and popular piety.

This last category contains a number of works which relate to Mary in one way or another. The *Protevangelium of James* was the first and most important. Written by an unknown author about A.D. 150, it relates many stories about Mary that have influenced art and literature ever since. According to the *Protevangelium*, Mary was born to aged parents, Joachim and Ann, who were of David's family. She was presented in the Temple at three years of age. As a young woman, she was engaged to Joseph, an elderly widower with children (the "brothers and sisters of Jesus"), after a miraculous sign indicated that he was favored by God. Jesus was born in a cave outside Bethlehem, and a midwife testified to Mary's virginity when she was accused of infidelity in giving birth to Jesus.

Scholars debate the historical value of the *Protevangelium of James*. Most seem to view the nonbiblical details as legendary. However, some Catholic specialists in Marian studies contend that the *Protevangelium* was accurate in stating that the "brothers and sisters" of Jesus were Joseph's children by a previous marriage. Other scholars disagree.

Many of the other apocryphal works about Mary and the hidden years at Nazareth depend on the *Protevangelium* as a source, and are far less valuable as literary works. Some were the "tabloids" of their time, inventing fictional miracles of the child Jesus and other legends, often in poor taste.

Other apocryphal literature expands upon the information given about Mary after Jesus began his public ministry. The fourth-century work, the *Gospel of Nicodemus*, adds details to gospel accounts of the Passion of Jesus, including Mary's meeting Jesus as he carried the cross to Calvary and Veronica's wiping the face of Jesus. These accounts were the background for the fourth and sixth Stations of the Cross. Several third- and fourth-century writings tell of the Assumption of Mary. They are not historical works, but they do show the belief of early Christians in the Assumption. Scattered through all the apocryphal writings are testimonies to the belief of early Christians in the intercessory power of Mary and in the importance of her role in God's plan for our salvation.

MARY IN LITERATURE:
THEOLOGIANS AND TEACHERS

Such doctrines as the virginity of Mary were declared by the earliest teachers of the Church. Before A.D. 110 Saint Ignatius of Antioch testified to the reality of the virgin birth and to the divinity of Jesus: "You are firmly convinced about our Lord, who is truly of the race of David according to the flesh, Son of God according to the will and power of God, truly born of a virgin" (cited in C 496).

Justin Martyr, A.D. 160, and Saint Irenaeus of Lyons, A.D. 180, also proclaimed the virgin birth and presented Mary as the new Eve, Mother of a new humanity redeemed by Christ (C 494). Saint Augustine expressed the belief of the fourth-century Church that Mary remained "always a virgin" (cited in C 510). Early teachers in the Eastern Church stated that Mary was "free from any stain of sin, as though fashioned by the Holy Spirit and formed as a new creature" (*Lumen Gentium* 59, cited in C 493). Saint Cyril of Alexandria led the movement at the Council of Ephesus (431) that proclaimed Mary as the Mother of God.

In the writings of these and other early Church teachers, we find evidence that the first Christians believed those truths about Mary later proclaimed as dogmas of our faith. As the Church grew and spread the gospel over all the earth, preachers and theologians continued to exalt Mary as the Mother of Jesus Christ and our Mother. Among the greatest of these were Saint Cyprian of Carthage (third century), Saint Athanasius of Alexandria, Saint Gregory of Nyssa, Saint Ephrem, Saint Ambrose, Saint Jerome (fourth century), Pope Saint Leo the Great, Saint Cyril of Alexandria (fifth century), Saint Romanos (sixth century), Saint Isidore of Seville (seventh century), Saint John Damascene (eighth century), Alcuin, Saint Paschasius (ninth century), John Geometer, Saint Odo, Saint Odilo (tenth century), Saint Anselm of Canterbury, Saint Peter Damian (eleventh century), Saint Bernard of Clairvaux (twelfth century), Saint Albert the Great, Saint Thomas Aquinas, John Duns Scotus (thirteenth century), Dante, Saint Bridget of

Sweden (fourteenth century), Saint Bernadine of Siena (fifteenth century), Saint Teresa of Avila, Saint Peter Canisius (sixteenth century), Francis Suárez, Saint John Eudes (seventeenth century), Saint Alphonsus Liguori (eighteenth century), Saint Louis de Montfort, John Cardinal Newman (nineteenth century), and all the popes of the twentieth century.

This list is by no means complete, but it shows that devotion to Mary and reflection on her place in redemption have always been important to Catholic teachers and writers. By studying their works, we can follow the development of Marian theology through the centuries. Catholic encyclopedias and some dictionaries of Mary (see Bibliography) list the authors named above, along with their major works.

MARY AND LIFE

In this chapter we have considered some of life's "meeting places" with Mary. Sacramentals, art, architecture, song, prayer, and literature are occasions and opportunities for us to encounter Mary. Such encounters may change the direction of our lives as they did for an arson squad detective, for parents praying for a healthy child, and for a young couple in search of a lasting marriage. Or they may deepen our understanding of God's love for us and of Mary's concern for our welfare.

In previous chapters we have seen that there are good reasons for devotion to Mary. We have studied the important place Mary has in Scripture and in the teaching and liturgy of the Church. We have examined the wonders of her appearances at various points in history.

In all these ways Mary has reached out to us. How shall we respond? One way is to imitate her virtues, a matter we will consider in the next two chapters. Another is to set regular prayer "appointments" with Mary, giving her the time and attention she needs to be an influence for good in our lives. The daily rosary can be just such an appointment, and we shall study this beautiful prayer in the last three chapters.

Questions for Discussion and Reflection

Have you heard stories about favors granted to those wearing a scapular or medal? Have you ever worn a scapular or medal in honor of Mary? Have you experienced favors which you've attributed to devotion to Mary? What is your favorite painting of Mary? your favorite sculpture? What artistic renditions of Mary do you have in your home? Have you ever visited churches dedicated in Mary's honor? Where? Have you participated in novenas in honor of Mary? Why do you think novenas are not as popular as in the forties and fifties? Do you think they should be promoted more by the Church? What is your favorite hymn in honor of Mary? your favorite prayer invoking Mary? Before reading this chapter, had you heard of the *Protevangelium of James?* What does it tell us about the devotion of early Christians to Mary?

This chapter included three stories of people who were helped by Mary in remarkable, though not miraculous ways. Has anything like the events in these stories ever happened to you?

Activities

Set up a little "shrine" in honor of Mary in your home. Put a statue or holy picture of Mary in a prominent place, and decorate it with flowers, a candle, or in any other way you like. For at least a week, let this shrine be a reminder to you of Mary, and say some prayer in her honor before the shrine once a day.

Meditate for at least half an hour on the place Mary has had in your life. Thank her for the special graces she has helped you receive, and ask her to bring you closer to Jesus in the years ahead.

Slowly and reflectively say the following prayer.

Angelus

The angel of the Lord declared unto Mary.
And she conceived of the Holy Spirit. Hail Mary…
Behold the handmaid of the Lord.
May it be done unto me according to your word. Hail Mary…
And the Word was made flesh.
And dwelt among us. Hail Mary…
Pray for us, O holy Mother of God,
that we may be worthy of the promises of Christ.
Let us pray: O Lord, it was through the message of an angel that we learned of the Incarnation of Christ, your Son. Pour your grace into our hearts, and by his Passion and cross bring us to the glory of his Resurrection. Through Christ, our Lord. Amen.

CHAPTER 8

MARY, MODEL OF VIRTUE

There is an old story about a hiker who was walking down a steep mountain trail. He stumbled on a rock and fell head-long over the edge of a cliff. Somehow he managed to grab a tree branch, saving himself from a long fall to the rocks beneath. Hanging there by both hands, he realized he couldn't climb back. In desperation, he called out, again and again, "Help, help! Is anybody up there?" Finally, he heard a mighty voice, "I'm up here. I'll help you. I'm God. But you'll have to trust me." "Thank you, God!" cried the hiker. "I trust you. I trust you." "That's good," replied God. "Now let go of that branch." There was a moment of silence. The hiker looked down to the rocks far below. Then he shouted, at the top of his lungs, "Is anybody else up there?"

It is very difficult to entrust ourselves to God! But sooner or later, at least at the moment of death, we have to "let go," knowing that we shall fall into God's hands, or into nothing at all.

That is why the *Catechism of the Catholic Church* begins with our profession of faith in God. We are made by God to know God, and our hearts will be restless until they rest in God. Our sins and this world's limitations will keep us from ever finding peace until we accept the salvation offered us by Jesus Christ. Our questioning minds will find the answers they seek only in the wisdom and light granted by the Holy Spirit. We must walk by faith.

Intimately linked to faith are hope and love. God has promised that we can find lasting happiness in perhaps the last place we would expect to find it—in death. Death, which appears to be the end of our existence, is actually a new beginning, the doorway to a life that never ends. But we cannot see through this doorway with our physical eyes, and so we must hope that what God has promised, God will accomplish for us.

The life and teachings of Jesus Christ reveal that God is Love. We exist because God wants to share love with us. The happiness we experience in human relationships provides us with a glimpse of the joy that can be ours when we open ourselves to the love of God and when we share that love with others. The fullness of this joy will come only when we see God face to face in heaven, but faith assures us that we will also find happiness even here on earth by loving God with our whole hearts, and by loving our neighbor as ourselves.

Faith, hope, and love are called "theological virtues" because they are gifts from God and govern our relationship to God. However, living by these virtues can be difficult. Doubts attack our efforts to believe in God and in God's promises. Fears chip away at hope, making us wonder if life after death might be only an illusion. Selfishness stifles love, blocking us from the realization that there is more happiness in giving than in receiving. Yes, it is so very hard to trust God and to let go of that branch!

A MODEL TO IMITATE

When doubts, fears, and selfishness assail us, it can be a great source of strength to realize we are not alone. To know that someone has walked the road we follow, and that the road leads home, can give us courage. In the enterprise of walking by faith, striving with hope, and living in love, Mary is a model who has gone before us. Her mortal life as Mother of Christ was one of faith, hope, and love. Today, as Mother of the

Church, she is a companion who helps us to believe, to trust, and to care.

Mary is also a model for the virtues of everyday life. She was a little girl who grew up to womanhood. She had the same hopes and dreams as we do. She enjoyed the beauty of nature and the companionship of those she loved. She formed opinions about such matters as justice and God's relationship to the weak and lowly. As a married woman, she had to get up in the morning and take care of her home, feed her family, do the laundry, get along with neighbors, go shopping, make plans. She knew what it was to be poor, frightened, and alone. She had to endure separation from home and relatives, and put up with misunderstanding and criticism. She had to accept the death of her husband and witness the brutal execution of her son. She adjusted to changing circumstances and widened her horizons to welcome into her life those who were, as members of the Church, the Mystical Body of Jesus.

Finally, after living in perfect love, without sin, Mary was brought to the glory of heaven by her son. And so we, who are followers of Christ, raise our eyes to Mary, "who shines forth to the whole community of the elect as a model of the virtues" (*Dogmatic Constitution on the Church*, 65).

Whoever we are, whatever our circumstances, Mary can be for us a pattern of how we ought to live. We shall look first at how she exemplifies faith, hope, and love. Then we will examine some of the ways Mary models the virtues of everyday living.

MARY, MODEL OF FAITH

Imagine that you are a young Jewish woman, residing in an unimportant village in a small, insignificant country. An angel appears to you and asks you to be the Mother of God. How would you feel?

This actually happened to Mary. She must have wondered, *Am I dreaming? How could God possibly choose me for the greatest responsibility ever asked of a human being?* Once the angel Gabriel convinced her that the request was genuine, Mary had to make an incredible leap of faith. "Yes, I accept. I do not know what the future holds, but I put my trust in God. If God, who created the world and knows all things, deems me worthy and capable, then I am God's servant."

"Faith is the theological virtue by which we believe in God and all that God has said and revealed to us...because [God] is truth itself" (C 1814). Mary accepted what she heard from Gabriel because its truth was guaranteed by God. No wonder the *Catechism of the Catholic Church* (C 148) calls Mary the "perfect embodiment of faith"! No wonder the Bible praises Mary for her faith: "And blessed is she who believed that there would be a fulfillment of what was spoken to her by the Lord" (Luke 1:45). We know from our vantage point in time that God has done great things through Mary, but Mary could not see the future. She could only put her faith in God.

The Bible tells of signs that accompanied the birth of her son: angels, shepherds, a star, wise men from the East. Such wonders must have reinforced her faith. But her faith soon had to light a path through darkness. First came the announcement of Simeon in the Temple: "This child is destined for the falling and rising of many in Israel, and to be a sign that will be opposed so that the inner thoughts of many will be revealed— and a sword will pierce your own soul too" (Luke 2:34-35). Mary realized then that her son would face bitter opposition, and that she would have to suffer. What Simeon foretold began immediately: efforts against the life of Jesus, exile to a foreign land, return, adjustment to a new home.

Then followed years of routine and ordinariness. As Mary changed diapers, taught her child to speak and read, watched him grow and work and play, it must have taken great faith for her to see in Jesus the "Son of the Most High" (Luke 1:32). The routine was broken by a traumatic experience when Jesus, at the age of twelve, was lost in Jerusalem. After Mary and Joseph found him in the Temple, they asked why he had left them in such anxiety. His response that he had to be in his Father's house puzzled them; "they did not understand what he said to them" (Luke 2:50). No human being could completely understand the mystery of the Incarnation, for no one knew Jesus totally except the Father (Matthew 11:27). Mary had to walk by faith without knowing all the answers or seeing everything perfectly.

After Jesus began his public ministry, Mary must have been pleased to hear of his mighty words and works. But then came criticism and resistance from religious and civil leaders. Through the good times and the bad, Mary believed. Even when she stood at the cross of Jesus, she kept faith, faith so strong that Jesus could entrust to her the task of being a mother to his beloved disciple. Through it all, Mary "never ceased to believe in the fulfillment of God's word. And so the Church venerates in Mary the purest realization of faith" (C 149).

Mary helps us believe in the presence and promises of God in the great events of life and the insignificant, in the triumphs and the tragedies. What we rejoice in or suffer through, Mary has celebrated or endured. By faith she prevailed. She has marked out a path of faith in God, and we can follow in her footsteps. When we doubt and waver, we can turn to her for the courage and strength we need to believe and to trust (*Dogmatic Constitution on the Church*, 65).

MARY, MODEL OF HOPE

"Hope is the theological virtue by which we desire the kingdom of heaven and eternal life as our happiness, placing our trust in Christ's promises and relying not on our own strength, but on the help of the grace of the Holy Spirit" (C 1817). The Bible presents Mary as a model of hope. She could say that all generations would call her blessed only because she had hope of eternal happiness. She relied not on her own strength, but on God her Savior, the Mighty One (Luke 1:47-49). She became Mother of Jesus Christ by the grace of the Holy Spirit (Luke 1:35), and she prayed for the coming of the Spirit upon the Church (Acts 1:14).

Every situation in Mary's life that required faith also demanded hope. "Faith is the assurance of things hoped for" (Hebrews 11:1). Mary had to hope that the angel's promises to her would be fulfilled. She had to hope that she, Joseph, and Jesus would return safely from exile in Egypt. She had to hope, as she pondered Jesus' enigmatic answer after he was found in the Temple, that God would somehow help her understand. She had to hope, as she stood at the foot of the cross, that life would overcome death. She had to hope that Jesus would bring her through the trials of this life to the joy of heaven.

Mary's hopes were realized. And the greatest sign of their fulfillment is her Assumption. Her glory in heaven pledges that Christ brings eternal life to all who put their hopes in him. So for generations of believers, Mary has been a Mother of holy hope. She encourages us today to put our trust in God's promises, to accept the salvation won for us by Jesus, and to rely on the help of the Holy Spirit.

MARY, MODEL OF LOVE

Love is the "theological virtue by which we love God above all things for [God's] own sake, and our neighbor as ourselves for the love of God" (C 1822). God is the source of love; we are able to love because we are first loved by God. Mary was loved as mother by Jesus, who is God! Her capacity for love had to be boundless, and the love she poured out on Jesus must surely have been the greatest maternal love ever known. Jesus was infinitely lovable, and his goodness constantly elicited even more love from Mary. There can be no doubt, therefore, that Mary's love for God the Father, Son, and Holy Spirit was greater than that of any other saint.

Mary's love for Jesus is not explicitly mentioned in the New Testament. It is taken for granted, or implied in such incidents as Mary's anxious search for Jesus when he was lost on the pilgrimage to Jerusalem. It was Mary's great love for Jesus that impelled her to stand at the foot of his cross. Mary, by her presence at the cross, joined her will to that of her son and participated in his sacrifice. When Jesus commended himself into the hands of his Father, Mary must have freely entrusted her son into the hands of the Father as well. Jesus said that there could be no greater love than his in giving his life for his friends. Mary's love, flowing from her son's love and united to it, was a mirror of his.

Mary's special relationship to the Holy Spirit is another assurance of her great love for God. It was the grace of the Holy Spirit that overshadowed her, causing her to conceive Jesus in her womb. The greatest gift of the Spirit is love (1 Corinthians

13), and this gift was granted to Mary in the person of Jesus and in her ongoing relationship to the Holy Spirit.

Because Mary was so loved by God, and because she loved God in return, she also loved God's children, her brothers and sisters. She displayed this love as soon as Christ was conceived. Mary, having heard from Gabriel that her cousin Elizabeth was expecting, went to visit her. Mary's love for Elizabeth is reflected in her cousin's delight when Mary appeared at her door. Mary assisted Elizabeth in the last three months of her pregnancy, a thoughtful and practical act of love. Mary demonstrated loving concern for others at the wedding feast of Cana. She noticed that the wine was running short, and she cared enough to do something about it.

The clearest evidence of Mary's love for others may be seen at Calvary. Christ's love was so intense that he could show concern for his beloved disciple, even while dying on the cross. Mary's love was so vast that Jesus could entrust to his Mother the beloved disciple, and disciples of every age, knowing that she would love them as her own!

MARY, MODEL OF PRUDENCE, JUSTICE, FORTITUDE, AND TEMPERANCE

Just as the theological virtues of faith, hope, and love have a special importance in Catholic tradition because they govern our relationship to God, so the four "moral" virtues of prudence, justice, fortitude, and temperance are significant because they regulate so much of human life. In fact, they are called the "cardinal" virtues (from the Latin word for "hinge"), because so many other virtues "hinge" on them. They are virtues for everyday living.

It is possible to gain some understanding of the moral virtues from a textbook. But it is much easier to live them when we have a model like Mary to imitate. Prudence, justice, fortitude, and temperance take on form and personality in Mary. These virtues leave the printed page and come to life in Nazareth, Bethlehem, Cana, and Jerusalem.

Prudence is the virtue that helps us do the right thing in any circumstance. Mary in the gospels is a wise, sensible woman, never naive or reckless. When Gabriel appeared to her, she asked questions to make sure she understood what God wanted. Only then did she give her reply. When faced with the difficult situation of how to approach Joseph with the fact of her pregnancy, she gave herself time to think and pray by going to visit Elizabeth. When confronted with behavior she could not understand, as when Jesus disappeared for three days, she did not fly into a rage. Instead, she expressed her emotions honestly. When Jesus' answer left her confused, she did not scold or nag, but reflected and prayed about the situation. Mary teaches us how to approach life prudently, calmly, prayerfully, always seeking God's will and the good of others.

Justice is the virtue which enables us to give God and others their due. It governs relationships between individuals and between segments of society. Mary's hymn, the *Magnificat*, teaches us to give God credit for the good that happens in life (Luke 1:46-50). Mary's hymn sets the tone for Luke's Gospel in proclaiming God's desire that justice be shown to the poor and the lowly. Luke's portrayal of Mary shows that the early Church saw in her a woman who was not afraid to call for justice. For Mary, God was a mighty ruler who would scatter the proud and bring down the powerful, lift up the lowly, and satisfy the needs of the hungry (Luke 1:51-53). Jesus loved the poor and demanded justice and mercy for them (Matthew 25:31-46). Following Jesus, the Catholic Church seeks justice for all. "The Church's love for the poor...is part of her constant tradition" (C 2444). Mary, Mother of the Church, teaches us to give to God what is God's and to treat people, especially the poor and lowly, as Jesus did.

Fortitude strengthens us to weather the difficulties and temptations of life. Mary was a woman of courage and strength who overcame every difficulty and temptation. As a young woman, she bravely set out on a difficult journey over dangerous roads to visit Elizabeth. She went to Bethlehem with Joseph when she was nine months pregnant. She endured exile in Egypt. She put up with the inconveniences associated with making annual pilgrimages to Jerusalem. Above all, she had the courage to stand at the cross of her son, enduring with him the taunts and mockery of his enemies. Mary teaches us to face life bravely, to endure inconvenience without complaint, to be dauntless in pursuing God's will no matter what the cost.

Temperance helps us control our desires and use the good things of life well. Mary controlled her desires because she submitted her will entirely to God's: "Here am I, the servant of the Lord" (Luke 1:38). She and Joseph were poor, making the offering of the poor (Leviticus 12:6-8) when they presented Jesus in the Temple. This means that they accepted the diet, lodging, and circumstances of the poor—a lifetime of controlling their desires. Yet Mary could find joy in the good things of life. She exulted in her relationship with the Almighty. She could appreciate simple pleasures, including fine wine, as is clear from the request she made to Jesus at the wedding feast of Cana. She teaches us that temperance means both moderation and appreciative use of God's gifts.

MARY, MODEL OF HUMILITY

It has been said that pride is at the root of all sin, for sin is the refusal to submit one's will to God. Sin should be spelled "s-I-n," for it means that I set myself and my choices against those of God and others. Adam and Eve are presented in the Bible as individuals who refused to accept God's word and authority. Their sin of pride was countered by Mary's humility in submitting to God, for she was God's servant in everything.

Mary shows that humility means recognizing the good in ourselves, all the while realizing that God makes it possible. Mary knew the exalted role she played in God's plan; no false humility for her! But she acknowledged that it came from God. "Surely, from now on all / generations will call / me blessed; / for the Mighty One has done great things for me" (Luke 1:48-49).

Mary teaches that humility does not mean thinking poorly of ourselves. Instead, it means thinking so much of God and others that we do not worry about ourselves. Mary found self-acceptance and happiness in giving herself to God's service and to caring for others. Adam and Eve show that pride is excessive focus on oneself. Mary demonstrates that humility is an expression of love of God and neighbor.

MARY, MODEL OF OBEDIENCE

The *Catechism of the Catholic Church* and the Bible note the close connection between faith and obedience. Faith is obedience to God's invitation to us as friends (C 142-143). Scripture speaks of "the obedience of faith" (Romans 1:5) and "Mary is its most perfect embodiment" (C 144). "The knot of Eve's disobedience was untied by Mary's obedience" (Saint Irenaeus, cited in C 494).

Faith inspired Mary to obey God's invitation to become the Mother of Jesus Christ. She stands as a model of obedience for us, and we imitate her when we respond to God's every wish as she did: "Here I am, the servant of the Lord; let it be with me according to your word" (Luke 1:38).

Mary, by her words at Cana, teaches us to obey Jesus: "Do whatever he tells you" (John 2:5). These words have echoed down through the centuries, and they are at the heart of all Marian apparitions approved by the Church. "Obey my son," Mary assures us, "and you will find life and peace."

MARY, MODEL OF LIFE IN THE SPIRIT

Paul writes that those who belong to Jesus Christ die to sin and live by the Holy Spirit. "If we live by the Spirit," he comments, "let us also be guided by the Spirit" (Galatians 5:25). Every Christian is invited to be a "temple of the Holy Spirit" (1 Corinthians 6:19), to spend each day in God's presence through the grace poured out by the Holy Spirit.

The effects of the Spirit's grace in our lives have traditionally been expressed as the *gifts* of the Holy Spirit. These are wisdom, understanding, counsel, fortitude, knowledge, piety, and fear of the Lord (Isaiah 11:2; C 1831). The results of the Holy Spirit's love in our hearts are called *fruits* of the Holy Spirit. They are charity, joy, peace, patience, kindness, goodness, generosity, gentleness, faithfulness, modesty, self-control, and chastity (Galatians 5:22-23; C 1832). The gifts and the fruits of the Holy Spirit are qualities that can help us lead happy, loving, and worthwhile lives.

These listings are not complete categories of virtues, and

some of them are "duplicates" of the theological and moral virtues. But they do provide time-tested ways of viewing qualities which are essential to those who want to imitate Jesus. Their designation as "gifts" and "fruits" of the Holy Spirit reminds us that the Christian life is not a solitary venture. It is instead union with God. It is openness to the grace of God, the saving presence of Jesus, and the love of the Holy Spirit. It is striving to do the right thing with the help of God.

Mary's special relationship with the Holy Spirit testifies that the gifts and the fruits of the Spirit were present in her life. She had the wisdom to put God first. She sought understanding in prayer and reflection. She requested counsel from God's heavenly messenger. She withstood every trial with fortitude. She was filled with the knowledge that comes from Scripture, as evidenced in her *Magnificat*, so rich in Old Testament imagery. Her piety expressed itself in her prayer and in her yearly pilgrimages to the Temple. Her fear of the Lord was not "fright," but awe and reverence, which flowed from her awareness of God as the Mighty One who had done great things for her.

Mary's charity, kindness, goodness, and generosity were displayed in all the ways she showed love for others. Her joy and peace of soul found expression in the *Magnificat*. Her patience, gentleness, and faithfulness led her to the cross of Jesus and enabled her to join herself to his loving sacrifice. Her modesty, self-control, and chastity were so beautiful that God chose her to be the Virgin Mother of Jesus.

As we strive to "live in the Spirit," Mary shows us the way. When this world's wisdom urges us to abandon the teaching of the Bible and the Tradition of the Church, Mary shows us that the wisdom, knowledge, counsel, and understanding that come from God will never disappoint us. When we are tempted to walk away from God because of suffering or frustration, Mary stands as a beacon of fortitude, piety, and fear of the Lord.

When we need the loving qualities known as the fruits of the Holy Spirit, Mary brings them into focus. She assures us that charity, kindness, generosity, and the rest of the fruits are possible. They flourished in her life, and with the grace of the Holy Spirit they will grow in ours.

And Mary is a Mother who reaches out to us from heaven. Just as children turn to their mothers when they need reassurance, so we can depend on Mary to be near us. We can look to her for strength and support.

"LET GO"..."LET IT BE"

At the moment of death, we must let go of every material thing we have clung to in this life. This ought not to be an act of desperation, but a decision we make because we believe God's word, hope in God's promises, and long to abandon ourselves to God's love. "Let it be with me according to your word."

Questions for Discussion and Reflection

What are the circumstances in your life that most call for faith, hope, love, and prudence, justice, fortitude, and temperance? Where do you most need humility and obedience? What are the situations where wisdom, understanding, counsel, fortitude, knowledge, piety, and fear of the Lord can best help you? In what areas can charity, joy, peace, patience, kindness, goodness, generosity, gentleness, faithfulness, modesty, self-control, and chastity make you a better person?

Can you think of at least one example from Mary's life where she exemplifies each of the virtues and qualities named above? How can Mary help you grow in the practice of these virtues?

Activities

Meditate and pray for a week about each of the virtues listed in this chapter. On Sunday, reflect on the theological virtues. On Monday, the moral virtues. On Tuesday, consider humility and obedience. On Wednesday, the gifts of the Holy Spirit. On Thursday, the first six fruits of the Spirit. On Friday, the last six. Each day, consider how Mary practiced each of these virtues and qualities, and ask her help as you try to imitate her. On Saturday, meditate on how these virtues made Mary more like her son, and ask her to help you rely on the Father, Son, and Holy Spirit to make you more like Jesus.

9

MARY AND THE FAMILY

"When I was a little girl," said Kathy, "my mother used to let me help her make our favorite cake, a One-Egg Devil's Food. Before she took the cake out of the oven to place it on the cooling rack, she would say, 'Let's pray a Hail Mary so the cake doesn't stick in the pan.' Once I asked her, 'Is it okay to pray about something as little as that?' She explained that God loves us and cares about the smallest details of our lives, even the way a cake comes out of the pan."

How very true! Parents note the seemingly trivial things their children do. A first-grader's artwork is posted on the refrigerator. A sixth-grader's perfect spelling test appears on the family bulletin board. A third-grader has only one line in the Christmas play, but Mom and Dad attend and wait eagerly for that one line. If human parents can show so much concern for their children, God, whose love and solicitude are infinite, surely cares about us.

Jesus explains that our heavenly Father notices the death of a sparrow, then adds: "And even the hairs of your head are all counted" (Matthew 10:30). God is great enough to create our vast universe; God is great enough to pay attention to its smallest part.

It is important to realize this truth, for a good deal of life is made up of routine tasks. Family life, in particular, includes much that seems unimportant and repetitious: preparing meals, washing dishes, cutting grass, sweeping floors, wiping fingerprints from windows, doing laundry, repairing broken chairs, fixing damaged toys....The list of unremarkable things seems to stretch on endlessly, and many people become discouraged because their lives seem so ordinary.

We should often remember that Jesus spent most of his life in an ordinary home doing manual labor. The hidden years at Nazareth show that family life and everyday work are so important that the Son of God chose them as the best possible way to spend his first thirty years on earth!

The Mother of the Son of God spent her entire life within the confines of ordinary households. Joseph, her husband, worked as a carpenter and cared for her and Jesus. The lives of these three seemed so common that when Jesus came back to his hometown as a preacher, he was resented by those familiar with his origins (Mark 6:2-6).

Yet Jesus, Mary, and Joseph are honored as the Holy Family because they are images of the holiness of God. They show that what we think is routine and ordinary God considers very important indeed.

FAMILY CRISES

The gospels relate that the routine of Nazareth was preceded by one crisis after another. First came the appearance of Gabriel, who announced God's invitation that Mary become Mother of the Savior. Then Joseph had to anguish over the fact that his fiancé was pregnant. After his fears were calmed by an angel, he and Mary celebrated their wedding, no doubt with the expectation that the child would be born in their home. But a decree from Rome forced them to set out for Bethlehem as Mary neared the time of her delivery, and the only crib they could find for the Son of God was a manger. Not long after the birth of Jesus, Mary and Joseph had to flee from Herod into Egypt, taking Jesus down long, dangerous roads into the unknown.

These gospel accounts have provided comfort to believers for twenty centuries. Mothers and fathers worrying whether their child would be born healthy have turned to Mary and Joseph for assurance. Poverty-stricken parents, unable to provide all that their children needed, have looked to Mary and Joseph for the help to fill up with love what was lacking in material goods. Parents fleeing their homeland to escape war and persecution have sought solace from Mary and Joseph.

Every mother, no matter how ideal her circumstances, is faced with the realization that a sword will pierce her heart. She will feel the pain her child endures in the inevitable injuries of childhood, the bruised feelings of adolescence, the sorrows of parting, the shadow of death. She will experience the poverty of knowing that, try as she might, she cannot provide perfect security for her child in this uncertain world. Mothers who are close to Mary know that she has been through what they experience. They know she listens to their prayers and is always at their side.

VILLAGE LIFE IN NAZARETH

Once Mary, Joseph, and Jesus returned to Nazareth after King Herod's death, they settled into the routine of everyday village life. Nazareth was located about sixty miles north of Jerusalem on a ridge some thirteen hundred feet above sea level in the district of Galilee. Galilee contained a mix of Jews and foreigners, and was regarded by the city folk of Jerusalem as a second-class area (John 7:52). Nazareth was a farming community, lowly even by Galilean standards (John 1:46).

Probably several hundred families lived in Nazareth on a six-acre tract of land. Homes were made of stone or mud brick, and were small, with only one or two rooms. A door on leather hinges provided entry, and several window openings let in light and air. Furniture might include a low table, a few chairs, and storage boxes for family belongings. Roofs were flat and sturdily braced so that people could sleep there on hot nights.

Most people in Nazareth were farmers who owned land handed down from their ancestors. In their fields which circled the village, they cultivated wheat, barley, flax, and other crops.

On hillside plots they tended grapes, figs, and olives. Most families also planted a garden where vegetables and herbs were grown for the table. They kept chickens for eggs and meat; goats and sheep for milk, wool, and an occasional feast; and a donkey or ox as a beast of burden.

Several homes might cluster around a courtyard where women would gather to grind grain on small millstones or bake bread in a communal oven. There they would perform many other household tasks, such as spinning thread, weaving cloth, and making garments. There, too, small children could play with balls, tops, hoops, dolls, and other toys under the watchful eyes of their mothers.

Farmers generally left their homes early to work the fields, assisted by their older children. Artisans worked in open shops connected to the home. Merchants conducted business at home or in a large courtyard near the center of the village.

A carpenter like Joseph would have plenty of work making yokes, carts, and tools for farmers, furniture for homes, and implements needed for daily living. On a typical day, Joseph would rise with the sun. After prayer and a bite to eat, he would work in the shop, using tools like hammers, saws, planes, and drills. Mary would be kept busy cooking, cleaning, drawing water at the village well, making clothing, and performing other household tasks (Proverbs 31:10-27). Before noon they would pray and share a light meal, then return to their tasks. Sunset brought them together for prayer and a substantial supper of cheese, bread, eggs, vegetables, olives, nuts, wine, and perhaps fish or chicken. As darkness fell, they offered evening prayer, then retired, lying on mats placed on the floor and covering themselves with cloaks or blankets.

As a little boy, Jesus joined other children at their games and helped his mother around the house. He watched Joseph work at the carpenter's bench, and when old enough, he began to work as an apprentice with Joseph. In time he became a carpenter, laboring alongside his foster father.

The family no doubt kept a garden, and might also have owned land where they planted grain and tended olive trees and grapevines. Joseph and Jesus helped farmers at harvesttime and other occasions when extra hands were needed. They co-operated with the village blacksmith to produce iron-tipped plows and other tools. They bartered their products for goods, such as pottery, sandals, food, animals, and some coinage.

Carpentry was a necessary and respected occupation in a village like Nazareth. But Joseph and Jesus would not have become wealthy from their profession. They could not charge high prices, for their customers were poor. One fourth of their annual income had to be paid in taxes to the Roman government. They tithed to the Temple in Jerusalem and paid other temple taxes. What was left could not have been much. Joseph and Mary had made only the offering of the poor, two turtle doves, when they presented the infant Jesus in the Temple.

Village people had to toil from sunup to sundown to make a living. But once a week the Sabbath brought respite. Every Friday evening, three blasts of a ram's horn would announce the beginning of the Lord's Day, and the villagers would gather at the synagogue for prayer and Scripture, returning home after services for a festive dinner. On Saturday morning there were more prayers and Bible readings at the synagogue. The remainder of the day was devoted to rest and relaxation.

At regular intervals during the year, Jewish festivals like Hanukkah and Passover provided opportunities for celebration and breaks from the ordinary routine. Luke reports that Jesus, Mary, and Joseph went to Jerusalem each year for the Passover. Such trips to the "big city" were special occasions for prayer and worship, for sightseeing and visiting friends.

Joseph, Mary, and Jesus found joy in sharing meals together, in their prayers, and in studying the Scriptures. They attended wedding parties and other village celebrations. Jesus' preaching reveals that he learned from Mary and Joseph to appreciate the simple things of life: bread baking, wheat and grapes and figs and olives, wildflowers shimmering in the sunlight, a hen gathering her chicks under her wings, a lamb lost and found, a sleepy-eyed fox emerging from its den, hard work and peaceful rest, the security of a child in mother's arms, the fun of conversation, the pleasure of sharing good food with friends. And flowing through each moment and every experience were love from others and love from God, love for one's companions and love for God who had created the world and made it very good.

WHAT WE LEARN FROM NAZARETH

We ought not idealize the hardships of village life or try to turn back the calendar to the first century. Conditions were primitive, amenities were few, privacy was minimal, the political situation was uneasy. It is a mark of Mary's greatness that amid such circumstances she could revel in the great things God had done for her!

But we can learn some very important lessons from Mary's life at Nazareth. The first is the one which began this chapter. Even the most routine tasks are important in God's eyes and provide a pathway to the greatest possible holiness. Mary spent her days serving the needs of Jesus and Joseph, cooking and cleaning, spinning thread and making clothes, drawing water and tending a garden. When mothers today get tired and frustrated at the many routine tasks they must continually perform ("Sometimes I think I'll go crazy if I have to wipe one more smudge off the wall," a mother once told me), they can think of Mary. Her life and example show that such everyday tasks have great significance. She points to the words of Scripture: "So, whether you eat or drink, or whatever you do, do everything for the glory of God" (1 Corinthians 10:31).

A second lesson is that Mary teaches us to attend to the importance of love in the family and in everyday relationships. Today much emphasis is placed on one's career and one's dealings outside the home—social obligations, school activities, civic organizations, sports, and exercise. These things can be good, but they ought not blind us to what comes first. If parents fail to love each other with tenderness, if they do not give their children time and affection, all else becomes meaningless. It has been observed that no one on a deathbed has ever said, "I wish I had devoted less time to my family and more to my business." God offers love to a child first and foremost through the mother and father, and this enables the child to love others. Jesus had the greatest possible love for others, a sure sign that he had been loved deeply at home. Mary's love for Jesus was the most significant human building block of that love which saved the world. She stands as a sign for the ages that the love of parents for their children is one of the most powerful forces on earth.

Third, Mary, Joseph, and Jesus teach us how much God loves the poor. Jesus showed a special affinity for the poor. He called them blessed (Luke 6:20). He asked us to be attentive to their needs (Luke 16:19-31). He identified himself with the poor (Matthew 25:40). Mary, who lived in poverty and proclaimed that God lifts up the lowly, echoes her son's wish that we care for the poor.

Fourth, Mary invites us to meditate upon Nazareth. She "treasured all these things in her heart" (Luke 2:51). Like her, we should reflect on the first thirty years of Christ's life. There are few lines in the Bible about these years, but there is much between the lines. The lessons drawn here from Nazareth are only the beginning of what we can learn from meditating on that little home where Jesus grew from infancy to adulthood. Such meditation can be an important means by which we come to "the knowledge of the Son of God, to maturity, to the measure of the full stature of Christ" (Ephesians 4:13).

LIKE MOTHER, LIKE CHILD

One of the adventures of being Christian is the quest for this "knowledge of the Son of God." "I want to know Christ," wrote Paul (Philippians 3:10). Mary, the Mother of Jesus, can help us in this quest.

Paradoxically, this happens when we learn about Mary from Jesus. The genetic structure which formed the human body of Jesus came from his Mother. He began his human life in her womb. He learned to speak and to pray with her accent. He related to God and to others with emotions modeled on hers. His human qualities and virtues were developed under Mary's tutelage and example. His great love of God and of others, his desire for friendship and companionship, his affection for children, his concern for the sick and afflicted, his gentleness and fiery dedication, his compassion and sense of justice, his imaginative use of language and parable, his conviction that good triumphs over evil and that life conquers death—these and so many of the other traits that make up the personality of Jesus Christ were nurtured in the home at Nazareth, primarily under the influence of Mary. (Joseph was an important influence too, but in this book we are focusing on Mary.) So from what we know of Jesus, we can infer a great deal about his Mother.

Beneath Jesus' longing to do the Father's will, we discover Mary's desire to be the servant of the Lord. In Jesus' readiness to bear the hardships of his mission, we see his Mother's patience in enduring the poverty of village life. Under Jesus' care for the poor lies the foundation of Mary's awareness that God lifts up the lowly and fills the hungry with good things. Before his courageous endurance of the cross came Mary's quiet acceptance of the sword of sorrow. As the purity in a pool of water tells us about the purity of its source, so the personality of Jesus speaks volumes about the personality of his Mother.

As we see Mary more clearly in the light of Christ's life and personality, so we understand Jesus better in the context of his relationship to Mary. Seeing Jesus as son of Mary helps us know him as one like us in every respect except sin (Hebrews 2:17; 4:15).

It also helps us grow in the likeness of Jesus. When we consider how the personality of Jesus was formed at Nazareth under the guidance of his Mother, we learn how to become more like him, developing gradually, as he did, "in wisdom and in years, and in divine and human favor" (Luke 2:52).

Mary invites us to her home. She suggests that we treasure the details of family life at Nazareth and ponder them in our heart. If we accept her invitation, we shall find a way of prayer that is both fascinating and useful. In Mary's company we will acquire some of her love for Jesus. We will, as her children, become more like her Son. We will "grow up in every way...into Christ" (Ephesians 4:15).

MARY'S LAST YEARS

The routine of Nazareth ended when Jesus began his public life. John's Gospel shows that Mary played an important role at Cana where Jesus performed his first miracle and at Calvary when Jesus gave his life for our salvation. Scripture does not describe Mary's emotions as she stood at the foot of the cross. But if we imagine someone we love hanging in agony on a cross, we will discover in our own feelings something of what Mary must have felt.

The gospels do not tell of Jesus' appearance to Mary after his Resurrection. In the Resurrection accounts, the evangelists named witnesses who could give objective testimony to the fact that Jesus had risen, and they judged that Jesus' own Mother would be seen as biased in his favor. To catch a glimpse of Mary's joy at her reunion with her risen son, however, we might picture her saying the *Magnificat* on Easter Sunday. Luke wrote his gospel long after the Resurrection, and no doubt he intended this hymn of praise to reflect Mary's feelings at all the "great things" God had done, and of these the greatest was the Resurrection.

Mary waited with the apostles and other believers for the coming of the Holy Spirit at Pentecost (Acts 1:13-14). By her presence and prayer, she helped bring to birth the Church as the Body of Christ, just as she had brought Jesus to birth more than thirty years before. The scattered traditions about Mary's last years do not provide us with certain historical information; one such tradition states that she spent these years in Ephesus with the apostle John. We can be sure that she prayed for the Church and shared her faith, hope, and love with the first believers.

Her mortal life ended with her Assumption, a glorious reunion with her son. Her coronation as Queen symbolizes the fact that Mary is Mother of Christ's family, the Church.

MARY AND TODAY'S FAMILY

The *Catechism of the Catholic Church* describes the family as the "domestic church" (*Familiaris Consortio* 21, cited in C 2204) and "the original cell of social life" (C 2207). The health of the family is essential both to the upbuilding of the Church and the survival of society. But the family is under great stress today. Divorce rates are high, abortions are routine, teenage delinquency is rampant, spousal battery and child abuse are common.

The remedy for such problems is a return to the values cherished by the Holy Family, especially love, fidelity, and commitment. We cannot heal all the ills of society overnight, but we can dedicate ourselves to these values. And as parents strive to live in love, fidelity, and commitment, they will find in Mary a perfect model to imitate.

Love is the decision to revere God with all our heart and to care for others as we care for ourselves. Love counters the self-centeredness that makes us want to put our own concerns above those of others. It causes us to dedicate ourselves to the will of God and the care of others. Mary's love can be seen in her readiness to be God's servant and in her complete dedication to her son. Parents who strive to imitate Mary's love will keep God's commandments and try to do God's will in everything. They will realize that in caring for their children, they are caring for Jesus. Their priorities will be those set by the Scriptures: God, spouse, and family.

Mary is a model of fidelity, a virtue often ridiculed in today's media. Promiscuity is portrayed in movies and television as glamorous, but in real life it brings misery and shame to both its perpetrators and its victims. Famous politicians and religious leaders have been disgraced by their own sins. Innocent spouses and children have been done irreparable harm when infidelity has shattered the stability of the home. Faithfulness may be ridiculed, but it is never outdated. Mary remained ever faithful to her commitments. Today's society will find stability only when all people imitate Mary's fidelity.

Mary teaches commitment, which is dedication to what has been promised, no matter what the cost. Too many people enter marriage or other vocations with the idea, "I'll stick to it as long as it makes me happy." This is a certain recipe for failure. No matter what vocation we choose, we will encounter hardships and difficulties. When Mary said yes to God at the Annunciation, she said yes to everything that would follow, the sorrow as well as the joy. She remained committed to her promises through the trials that followed Christ's birth, the routine of Nazareth, and the agony of Calvary. Her example teaches us to be committed to the promises we make to God and to others.

Mary was faithful and committed because she truly loved God and the people in her life. In her love, fidelity, and commitment, we find qualities which will restore health to families, Church, and society.

PATRONS OF A HAPPY DEATH

As we conclude these reflections on Mary and the family, we should consider the role of the Holy Family at the moment of our death. A traditional prayer invokes the Holy Family:

Jesus, Mary, and Joseph, I give you my heart and my soul.
Jesus, Mary, and Joseph, assist me in my last moments.
Jesus, Mary and Joseph, may I breathe forth my soul in
   peace with you.

The Bible implies that Joseph died before Jesus began his public ministry. He must have died in the presence of Jesus and Mary. A more blessed death cannot be imagined. In the prayer cited above, Catholics have long asked for the happiness of dying in the company of Jesus, Mary, and Joseph.

My sister, Joann, often said this prayer with my mother during her last illness. When Joann visited Mom on the Sunday after Christmas, Mom said, "They're coming." Joann wasn't sure what these words meant, but their meaning became apparent when Mom died gently that afternoon. She had often asked for the grace to breathe forth her soul in peace with Jesus, Mary, and Joseph. On the morning of her death, she saw them coming to assist her in her last moments. She died, I believe, in their arms, for that Sunday after Christmas was the Feast of the Holy Family.

Mary was present not only at the death of Joseph, she was also present at the death of her son on Calvary. That is why we Catholics call upon her with the words, "Holy Mary, Mother of God, pray for us sinners, now and at the hour of our death."

MARY CARES

In life's ordinary moments, in simple tasks like taking a cake from a pan, Mary cares and teaches us that God cares too. In life's greatest moments, including the hour of our death, Mary cares and helps us experience the love of Jesus. Because she was Mother of the family at Nazareth, she is Mother of the Church today. She will be Mother of Christ's family forever in heaven.

Questions for Discussion and Reflection

Have you ever prayed about something as unimportant as a cake coming out right? Do you believe God cares about such things?

Have you ever felt that your life seemed routine and unimportant? Have you considered how much time Mary, Joseph, and Jesus spent in ordinary family life and routine tasks? Does reflecting on the life of the Holy Family in Nazareth help you see your own life in a different way?

Time spent thinking about the hidden years at Nazareth can produce interesting insights into the gospels. In Matthew 11:30 Jesus says, "My yoke is easy." Carpenters of Jesus' time frequently made yokes for oxen, and there is a charming tradition that Jesus' saying originates from his experience as a yoke-maker at his Nazareth shop where he had a sign, "My yokes fit easy." Can you name other sayings and parables of Jesus that reflect his background in Nazareth?

The text lists some lessons we can learn from Mary at Nazareth. Can you think of any others? Do you agree that we can learn much about Mary from Jesus, and much about Jesus from Mary? Why or why not? What lessons for today's families would you draw from the life of the Holy Family at Nazareth?

Activities

Spend half an hour meditating on a typical day at Nazareth. Imagine yourself sharing the life of Jesus, Mary, and Joseph from morning until night. Try to picture village life as Mary might have lived it. Imagine the sights, smells, sounds, tastes, and textures of the carpenter shop, the home, and the family courtyard in Nazareth. Then talk to Mary about what her life was like and about your life today. Ask her to help you understand Jesus better through this meditation.

Say reverently the prayer to the Holy Family for a happy death. Then say a Hail Mary for the same intention.

10

MARY'S ROSARY: THE JOYFUL MYSTERIES

Some time ago I attended a day of prayer for priests. The topic for the day was the rosary, and during a discussion Father Jacob remarked, "The rosary is the Bible translated into prayer."

"The Bible translated into prayer." A better description of the rosary would be hard to find! The rosary takes the great mysteries of the Bible from the printed page and writes them on our hearts.

THE ORIGIN AND DEVELOPMENT OF THE ROSARY

There is a legend that Mary appeared to Saint Dominic early in the thirteenth century and gave him the rosary. This legend was apparently created by a Dominican preacher, Alan de la Roche, late in the fifteenth century. Several papal documents cite the story as piously believed, but do not vouch for its truth. Most modern historians of the rosary agree that the legend has no basis in fact.

The development of the rosary actually seems to have begun before Dominic as a form of prayer patterned on the Book of Psalms. Religious communities sang and prayed the psalms. Many laypeople wished to imitate them, but few could read. Before the twelfth century (perhaps as early as the eighth) someone came up with the idea of reciting the Lord's Prayer one hundred fifty times in lieu of the psalms. Those devoted to Mary would say the first part of the Hail Mary instead of the Lord's Prayer. People began counting the prayers with the help of beads strung on a cord. Sets of one hundred fifty prayers were called psalters. When divided into sets of fifty, they were known as chaplets.

Around the thirteenth century, the custom arose of applying the psalms to Jesus or Mary by adding to each psalm a New Testament verse. This custom was quickly adapted to the recitation of the chaplets in honor of Mary. At first, one event, like the Annunciation, would be named for consideration during the recitation of a chaplet, with emphasis on the "joys" of Mary. In the fourteenth century, devotion to the sufferings of Mary led people to reflect on her "sorrows." Later in the same century, meditation on the "glories" of Mary began. People might recite three chaplets, one joyful, one sorrowful, and one glorious. A chaplet of fifty Hail Marys came to be called a "rosarium" ("rose garden"), our "rosary," and this name gradually prevailed.

Early in the fifteenth century, the practice began of linking a phrase for meditation to each Hail Mary. Because this required the use of a book, it was soon simplified. A rosary of fifty Hail Marys was divided into five sets of ten, with each set (decade) separated by an Our Father. A mystery was assigned to each decade, so that only fifteen mysteries instead of one hundred fifty had to be memorized. The pattern of five Joyful, Sorrowful, and Glorious Mysteries, still in use today, was thereby established.

During the sixteenth century, fifteen mysteries became the norm. Also at this time, the prayers of the rosary were brought into their modern form. The second half of the Hail Mary was added, and the Prayer of Praise (Glory to the Father) was used to close each decade of the rosary. Pope Pius V officially approved this rosary in 1569. In 1573, he established the Feast of the

Rosary in thanksgiving for the victory of Christian Europe over Muslim forces in the battle of Lepanto on October 7, 1571.

Since the sixteenth century, different ways of introducing and closing the five decades of the rosary have been used. The structure usually followed in the United States today is given below. Since Mary's apparitions at Fatima, a prayer taught by Mary to the children is often recited after each decade: "O my Jesus, forgive us our sins, save us from the fires of hell, and lead all souls to heaven, especially those most in need of thy mercy."

Many popes since Pius V have praised the rosary and attached indulgences to its recitation. The popes of the nineteenth and twentieth centuries have been especially enthusiastic in their tributes to the rosary. The Dominican Order and other religious communities have fostered devotion to the rosary. Saints like Peter Canisius, Louis de Montfort, and Alphonsus Liguori have promoted it. Groups such as the Confraternity of the Most Holy Rosary (an organization dedicated to spreading devotion to the rosary) and parish rosary sodalities have also increased the popularity of the rosary. These and many other factors, including the inherent beauty of the rosary, have helped give it an honored place in Catholic spirituality.

PRAYING THE ROSARY

In the United States the rosary is commonly begun with the Sign of the Cross, the Apostles' Creed, one Our Father, three Hail Marys (usually for an increase of faith, hope, and charity), and one Prayer of Praise. Like the overture of a musical performance, these prayers set the tone and get us into the mood for the remainder of the rosary.

Next come the five decades. Each consists of an Our Father, ten Hail Marys, and a Prayer of Praise. Before each decade, a mystery is announced for meditation while the vocal prayers are said. After each decade, the Fatima Prayer, "O my Jesus" may be used.

The rosary is usually ended with the recital of the Hail, Holy Queen, a response verse, and closing prayer. The invocation, "Queen of the Most Holy Rosary, pray for us," may be repeated three times, followed by the Sign of the Cross.

The purpose of these vocal prayers is to calm our bodies and focus our minds on the heart of the rosary, meditation on the great mysteries of our faith. Most saints have recommended that we meditate (think in a prayerful way) about the life, death, and resurrection of Jesus, and apply his teachings to our life situation. However, many of us find it hard to concentrate when we attempt such reflection. Our minds jump from one distraction to another. We daydream. We wonder if it isn't time to do something else. The rosary helps solve such problems. Repetition of the vocal prayers tends to quiet us. Holding the beads reminds us that we are at prayer. The Prayer of Praise and the announcing of a new mystery help us refocus if our mind has wandered. The five decades measure the passage of time without our having constantly to check the clock.

The mysteries of the rosary place before us scenes from the gospels linked to our own lives and destiny. They are divided into five Joyful, five Sorrowful, and five Glorious Mysteries. The Joyful Mysteries are the Annunciation, the Visitation, the Nativity, the Presentation, and the Finding in the Temple. These are customarily used on Mondays and Thursdays, and on Sundays from Advent until Lent. The Sorrowful Mysteries are the Agony in the Garden, the Scourging at the Pillar, the Crowning With Thorns, Jesus Carries the Cross, and the Crucifixion. These are used on Tuesdays and Fridays, and on Sundays during Lent. The Glorious Mysteries are the Resurrection, the Ascension, the Descent of the Holy Spirit, the Assumption of Mary, and the Coronation of Mary. These are used on Wednesdays and Saturdays, and on Sundays from Easter until Advent.

MEDITATING ON THE MYSTERIES: THE ESSENCE

The most fundamental way of meditating on the mysteries of the rosary is to consider each event as described in the Bible and to enter into it. We picture the people involved, listen to their conversation, and watch the action. We imagine what they might see, hear, smell, taste, and touch. We feel their emotions. We envisage ourselves as participants.

This kind of meditation adds color and texture to our

understanding of the Bible. It draws us nearer to Jesus and his Mother. It leads us to prayerful attitudes of praise, thanksgiving, sorrow, and petition.

MEDITATING ON THE MYSTERIES: BIBLE BACKGROUND

We can enhance our understanding of the mysteries by considering other parts of the New and Old Testaments related to them. When we pray the rosary frequently, such consideration adds depth to our meditation. The rosary is "the Bible translated into prayer," and there is sufficient material in the Bible for a lifetime of prayer.

MEDITATING ON THE MYSTERIES: OUR LIFE

The *Catechism of the Catholic Church* states that meditation on what we read helps us "to make it our own by confronting it with ourselves. Here, another book is opened: the book of life." We consider what is written in the Bible and apply it to our own situation. Then we honestly ask, "Lord, what do you want me to do?" (C 2706).

Praying the rosary is a good way to relate what we read in the Bible to our own lives. As we meditate on the mysteries, we consider the actions of Jesus and Mary and see how we might follow their example. We thank God for successes and ask pardon for failures. We resolve to do better. In these and other ways, we open "the book of life" and allow God to fashion us in the image of Jesus Christ. As Mary was transformed by the Holy Spirit, so too are we. "And all of us...seeing the glory of the Lord...are being transformed into the same image from one degree of glory to another; for this comes from the Lord, the Spirit" (2 Corinthians 3:18).

MEDITATING ON THE MYSTERIES: INTERCESSION FOR THE CHURCH

The rosary can expand our spiritual horizons. We are followers of Christ, not just for our own salvation but for the salvation of others. We are called by baptism to share in the "common priesthood of all believers" (C 1268), to "participate in the apostolic and missionary activity of the People of God" (*Lumen Gentium* 11, cited in C 1270). One of the most effective ways to do this is prayer.

Jesus prayed for all those who would believe in him (John 17:20). Jesus asked that we pray even for enemies and persecutors (Matthew 5:44; Luke 6:28). Ephesians urges that we "always persevere in supplication for all the saints [members of the Church]" (6:18). James tells us to pray for one another because "the prayer of the righteous is powerful and effective" (5:16). Paul prayed constantly for others (2 Thessalonians 1:11), affirmed that early Christians prayed for one another (2 Corinthians 9:14), and implored the believers to pray for him (Colossians 4:3; 1 Thessalonians 5:25).

As followers of Christ, then, we must pray for others. Our obligation is more urgent today because modern communications alert us to the needs of people in every land. Closer to home, we are asked by friends and relatives to pray for them. The parish bulletin solicits prayers for couples planning to marry, for teens preparing for confirmation, for bereaved families. How can we attune ourselves to all these needs? How can we keep our promises to pray for others? The rosary!

Mary's rosary is effective as a prayer for others because Mary is Mother of the Church. She devoted her life on earth to bringing Christ to all people. She continues to intercede for them in heaven:

> This motherhood of Mary in the order of grace continues uninterruptedly from the consent which she loyally gave at the Annunciation and which she sustained without wavering beneath the cross, until the eternal fulfillment of all the elect. Taken up to heaven, she did not lay aside this saving office but by her manifold intercession continues to bring us the gifts of eternal salvation (*Lumen Gentium* 62, cited in C 969).

As we pray the rosary, we are inspired by Mary to pray with her for our brothers and sisters throughout the world. One effective way to do this is to let each mystery lead us to consider how it is relived in the world today. Mary's yes at the Annunciation calls to mind the many believers who are now trying to say yes as they choose a vocation in life. Praying the first joyful mystery can be a prayer of intercession for them. The agony of Jesus on the cross turns our attention to those who are persecuted today. The fifth sorrowful mystery is an opportunity to pray for them.

It is not necessary to add words to the vocal prayers of the rosary. We need only place people in the care of Mary and Jesus. We can do this, for example, by imagining a suffering friend standing beneath the cross of Jesus and being blessed by him (fifth sorrowful mystery). Or we might visualize a deceased friend being ushered by Mary into Christ's presence (fifth glorious mystery). We bring others to Jesus and Mary.

ESSENCE, BACKGROUND, LIFE, AND INTERCESSION

When we pray the rosary, we can use one of these four methods or join them in various combinations. I meditate on the biblical background only occasionally. Most often I consider the essence of a mystery during the Our Father and two Hail Marys. I use the next two or three Hail Marys to apply the mystery to my own life. I devote the rest of the decade to intercessory prayer.

In whatever way we meditate on the mysteries, we should feel free to follow where the Holy Spirit leads. The guidelines given here are intended as suggestions, not rigid rules.

The remainder of this chapter will offer meditation patterns for each of the Joyful Mysteries of the rosary. First, the essence of the mystery will be considered, then the biblical background, next possibilities for personal application, and finally ideas for intercessory prayer. Chapter Eleven will be devoted to the Sorrowful Mysteries, and Chapter Twelve to the Glorious Mysteries.

THE JOYFUL MYSTERIES

Christ came to bring joy to the world, as the angels announced at his birth (Luke 2:10; see John 15:11; 17:13). This joy is not to be confused with fun. It is rather the inner peace and happiness that flow from the Holy Spirit and the knowledge that we are God's children because we belong to Christ (Galatians 5:22-23).

In the Litany of Loreto, Mary is invoked as "cause of our joy." She is certainly that because she gave birth to Christ, turning the darkness of night into the brightness of God's glory (Luke 2:9). Her life stands as testimony to the truth of what Jesus promised: "Your hearts will rejoice, and no one will take your joy from you" (John 16:22).

Perfect joy, however, can come only in heaven. The Joyful Mysteries of the rosary show that joy on earth is not limitless. The Annunciation brought Mary the happiness of Christ's presence, and the awesome responsibility of caring for him. The Visitation gave Mary the joy of Elizabeth's company, but was followed by the problem of explaining her pregnancy to Joseph. The birth of Jesus summoned the joy of angels' song from heaven and the terror of Herod's wrath from hell. With Simeon's praise at the Presentation came his warning of a sword to pierce Mary's heart. The joy of finding Jesus in the Temple came at the cost of three days of anxious searching. These mysteries teach us on the one hand not to be surprised that our lives are imperfect, and on the other that joy is possible even in the midst of affliction.

THE FIRST JOYFUL MYSTERY— THE ANNUNCIATION

Luke 1:26-38

We picture Mary at prayer in a simple house in Nazareth. We set the scene as we imagine it might have been. We look at the plain furnishings of the room. We feel the coolness of the air. We hear children playing outside. We notice the smell of baking bread from an oven in the courtyard outside her home. Then we visualize the angel Gabriel appearing to her. We see the amazement on Mary's face as Gabriel says, "Greetings, favored one! The Lord is with you." We listen to the conversation, focusing especially on Mary's words, "Here am I, the servant of the Lord; let it be with me according to your word." We watch as the angel fades from Mary's sight. We ponder how Mary must have felt at the moment when the Holy Spirit descended and the Son of God began to dwell within her. We adore Jesus, the Word-made-flesh. We express our gratitude to Mary for her humble obedience which made possible our redemption.

∽o∽

The Bible background of the Annunciation includes the announcement of the birth of John the Baptist and its effect on John's parents, Zechariah and Elizabeth. Related to the Annunciation also are New Testament teachings on obedience to the will of God. Mary's words, "Let it be with me according to your word," call to mind the obedience of Jesus and the words of the Lord's Prayer, "Thy will be done."

Among the Old Testament passages connected to the Annunciation, the prophecy of Isaiah stands out: "Look, the young woman is with child and shall bear a son, and shall name him Immanuel" (7:14). Also important is the Daughter-Zion imagery of Zephaniah 3:14-17 and Zechariah 2:10-13 (see Chapter Three).

∽o∽

After we ponder Mary's humble obedience to God's will, and reflect on other Bible passages related to it, we should discern how this applies to us. Our particular vocation in life is a summons to say yes to God. A married person is asked to say yes generously to all the demands of family life. A priest or religious must respond positively to the call of ministry. A single individual can imitate Christ in a life of service and love.

All of us are faced with constant choices between right and wrong, good and evil. Do we say yes to what is right and good as Mary did? We examine our conscience, ask God's pardon for failures, thank God for the grace that has enabled us to succeed, and resolve to imitate Mary's generosity and obedience. (See also the reflections on faith and obedience in Chapter Eight).

∽o∽

We consider those who are now asked to say yes to God at important moments in their lives. Candidates for the priesthood and religious life are seeking to discern God's will. Young couples in marriage-preparation programs are trying to say "I do" forever. We place them in Mary's care and ask her to present them to her son, by whose grace alone they say, "Here am I, the servant of the Lord."

THE SECOND JOYFUL MYSTERY— THE VISITATION

Luke 1:39-56

We accompany Mary on her long journey from Nazareth to Ain Karim, the village of Elizabeth and Zechariah. After packing food, water, and clothing, and bidding her family goodbye, she joined a caravan to Jerusalem. Walking twenty miles a day through the lush farmland of Galilee, the grainfields and flocks of Samaria, and the rocky hills of Judea brought the caravan to Jerusalem in three days. Along the way, Mary made friends with other travelers, finding reassurance in the company of those who seemed eager to protect one so young and vulnerable. She chatted with others, prayed, and wondered what the future would bring.

From Jerusalem she joined another small group on their five-mile journey to Ain Karim. She must have wondered, "What if I was dreaming? What if Elizabeth is not pregnant?" Then just down the road was the house and... "Yes, it's Elizabeth! With a smile as big as she is! Oh, thank you heavenly Father!"

The two embraced. Mary's fears were washed away with the tears of joy that flowed from Elizabeth's greeting, "Blessed are you...and blessed is the fruit of your womb." Mary's response was a song of joy: "My soul magnifies the Lord."

Three months of visiting followed, of a young mother helping an older one. There were days of conversation and prayer, of studying Scripture, of looking to what the future would bring. Then Mary made the long journey home, still unsure of what to say to Joseph, but confident that God would guide her.

The scriptural background for the Visitation brings Joseph into the picture (Matthew 1:18-25). We can suppose that upon returning from her visit with Elizabeth, Mary met with Joseph and tried to explain. But he must not have been able to understand. Days went by. Joseph stopped seeing Mary and even speaking to her, until one morning he knocked at her door, an expression of amazed happiness on his face. "Last night I saw an angel," he said. "Let's visit the rabbi. We have arrangements to make!"

〜∞〜

An Old Testament parallel to Mary's *Magnificat* may be found in Hannah's song of joy at the birth of her son, Samuel (1 Samuel 2:1-10). The Second Book of Samuel (6:12-16), the account of David's bringing the Ark of the Covenant to Jerusalem, portrays David dancing and leaping for joy before the Ark. It is possible that Luke had this scene in mind when he wrote that John leaped for joy in his mother's womb. In any event, the Litany of Loreto invokes Mary as "Ark of the Covenant."

〜∞〜

The love, graciousness, and friendship that characterized the relationship between Mary and Elizabeth invite us to examine the place of these virtues in our lives. Does love for our family and friends take priority over all else? Are we gracious in showing hospitality to others? When we make social visits with friends and family, are we sincerely interested in them and in their lives? Are we polite during chance meetings with others and when answering the doorbell and telephone?

Mary dealt with the issue of her pregnancy prudently and prayerfully. She remained silent until she could visit with Elizabeth to seek reassurance and advice. She exemplifies the virtue of prudence and the importance of handling difficulties calmly and carefully.

Mary's *Magnificat* teaches us to praise and thank God for all blessings. It demonstrates true humility as well as concern for the poor and needy.

Mary was privileged to carry Christ within her body. We, too, receive Christ into our body in holy Communion. As we take holy Communion, do we have Mary's love and reverence for Jesus?

〜∞〜

Mary's long journey to Ain Karim reminds us of people today who are faced with misunderstanding and family problems. We place these people before Mary and ask her to join with us in praying for the Holy Spirit's gifts of prudence, wisdom, counsel, and understanding.

The real existence of Jesus and John in their mothers' wombs shows that unborn children are human beings. We entrust them to God's care, and we pray that all people may learn to respect every child's right to life.

THE THIRD JOYFUL MYSTERY— THE NATIVITY

Luke 2:1-21

Joseph led the small donkey he had purchased for hauling wood. Now it carried a far more precious burden. "Are you comfortable?" he asked his wife. She smiled weakly and nodded. They, like many in the caravan, were moving southward to register for yet another census. For Mary the trip meant three days of discomfort, for Joseph three days of worry that the baby would come before they arrived at their destination.

In Bethlehem they found no room at the inn. As Mary's time drew near, Joseph resolved that he would find a place with some shelter and privacy. He discovered a hillside cave where sheep huddled in bad weather. In this cave the Son of God was born. Mary held her child in her arms for a long time, then handed him to Joseph. "He's beautiful," Mary said, and Joseph agreed.

"May we come in?" asked the leader of the little group. "We're only poor shepherds, but God sent messengers to tell us of the birth of this child." "Come," said Joseph, "for God loves the poor. God loves every one of us."

We stand among the shepherds. The cave is small and there are unpleasant odors, but Joseph has spread clean straw on the ground under the manger where the baby lies. He smiles, invites us to step closer, and asks if we'd like to hold the child too. We take the child and know that our arms embrace God.

ഇൗ

With Luke's account of the Nativity stands the great passage of John 1:1-18. "In the beginning was the Word...and the Word was God.... And the Word became flesh and lived among us." Our meditation on the birth of Christ can include Paul's testimony to the Incarnation in Galatians 4:4-5, the hymn of Philippians 2:6-11 proclaiming that Christ "emptied himself...being born in human likeness," and Hebrews 1:1-4, stating that Christ is "the reflection of God's glory."

The Old Testament background for meditating on this mystery encompasses all the prophecies, especially those used during the Advent season. Notable is the prophecy of Isaiah chosen as the first reading for Christmas Midnight Mass: "The people who walked in darkness / have seen a great light..." (Isaiah 9:1-7).

∾

The fact that the Word was made flesh as a tiny child born to poor parents in humble surroundings is a lesson that God's ways are not our ways. How would we have responded to Joseph and Mary if they had come to us for assistance two thousand years ago? How do we respond to the poor and needy today?

Christ was born in Bethlehem. God became human. But the Incarnation continues today as Christ dwells in every human being. What we do to others, we do to Jesus. Do we recognize the presence of Jesus in the members of our families? in other people? Do we honestly try to treat others as we would treat Jesus himself?

Christ was poor and humble, as were Mary and Joseph. Do we imitate their humility? (See the reflections on humility in Chapter Eight.) Or do we demand preferential treatment? Are we resentful when we have to wait or are inconvenienced?

God entered the created world through the Incarnation. Jesus had a body like ours. He ate the food we eat, breathed the same air, drank our water. By becoming one of us, Jesus put the stamp of approval on created things. Do we appreciate the material world and all it contains as blessings from God? Do we remember that Christ shares our hopes and dreams, our joys and sorrows, our very existence? As a result of this fact, do we try to avoid pessimism and to do our best to bring the light of Christ into the world?

〜〜〜

As we meditate on this mystery, our prayer can encompass expectant parents, especially those who, like Mary and Joseph, have to face problems. We ask Mary and Joseph, who cared for Jesus and watched over him after he was born, to be near parents with small children. We think of those, like doctors and nurses, who care for children, and we ask Jesus to bless their efforts.

THE FOURTH JOYFUL MYSTERY— THE PRESENTATION

Luke 2:22-40

Mary held her precious burden carefully as she and Joseph walked through the Court of the Gentiles. They had taken their son to the rabbi for circumcision on the eighth day after his birth and had named him Jesus. Now they came to the Temple on the fortieth day to present him before the Lord (Exodus 13:2) and to perform the rites prescribed in Leviticus 12:1-8. The vast court was thronged with thousands of people. Stalls had been set up where pilgrims might purchase lambs and doves for sacrificial offerings. Joseph purchased two doves and proceeded with Mary to the Court of the Women.

After the ceremony had been completed, they stood quietly for a while, admiring the temple building with its gold ornamentation glistening in the sunlight. Suddenly, an old man hobbled over. "I am Simeon," he told them. With a gentle smile he took the child in his arms, lifted his eyes toward heaven and prayed in a strong voice, "Master, now you are dismissing your servant in peace, according to your word; for my eyes have seen your salvation..." As he handed Jesus back to Mary, his wrinkled hands trembled as he said to her, "This child is destined for the fall and rise of many in Israel...and a sword will pierce your own soul too." He had no sooner finished when an elderly woman introduced herself as Anna. She looked at Jesus and declared to the crowd attracted by the commotion, "Praise God. This child is the answer to the prayers of all those who have looked for salvation!"

〜〜〜

Luke, in his account of the Presentation, highlights the faithful obedience of Mary and Joseph to the law, as well as the fact that Christ came to save both Gentiles and Jews (2:32). Matthew does not mention the Presentation. He points to God's plan to save all people when he tells of the wise men who followed a star from the East to worship the newborn king. Their journey occasions Herod's massacre of the innocents and the flight of the Holy Family into Egypt. After Herod's death, the Family settles in Nazareth. Matthew 2:1-23, which recounts these events, may be considered during the fourth joyful mystery, as may the quiet years of Christ's early childhood in Nazareth which followed the return from Egypt.

Old Testament background of the Presentation includes Exodus 13:2 and Leviticus 12:1-8. These passages formulated the laws obeyed by Mary and Joseph when they brought Jesus to the Temple.

⌘

Mary and Joseph were obedient to the laws of God. Are we eager to obey God's law expressed in the Ten Commandments, the teaching of Jesus, and the commandments of the Church? Mary was courageous in accepting the sword which would pierce her heart. Are we courageous in facing the trials and sufferings that touch our lives?

⌘

This mystery provides us with an opportunity to pray that all people may come to know and respect God's laws, which alone can give order to our world. As Mary and Joseph present Jesus in the Temple, they remind us to pray for parents with hopes and dreams for the infants they put in God's care.

Simeon and Anna are biblical counterparts to the senior citizens of today, especially those in nursing homes, who long to see God's face. We pray that they may experience the peace and joy felt by Anna and Simeon as they held Jesus in their arms.

The sword which pierced Mary's heart has in some way pierced the heart of every parent whose child suffers from hunger, sickness, accident, physical defects, and mental disabilities. We ask that parents whose hearts are pierced with sorrow may be comforted and strengthened by their Mother in heaven.

THE FIFTH JOYFUL MYSTERY—
THE FINDING IN THE TEMPLE

Luke 2:41-52

Waves of panic washed over Joseph, submerging him in a flood of fear and doubt. "No, Mary," he said, "he's not with the men. I've looked everywhere. I thought he had left Jerusalem with the women and children and that he was in your group." Joseph saw the anguish in Mary's eyes and quickly went to her side. "We must return to Jerusalem right away," he told her. "We will find Jesus, I promise you. We will."

But as they left the caravan and walked silently down the road, Joseph's mind was full of dread. Was Jesus in Jerusalem or had he panicked and set out alone when he realized that his parents were gone? The roads were dangerous even for members of a caravan. A twelve-year-old boy would be a lamb among wolves. Jerusalem was not much safer. Jesus would be an ideal target for the slave trade. Joseph dared not express his fears to Mary as they hurried along. He only whispered, "Let's pray that God will protect Jesus. We must entrust him to God's care."

By the time they arrived in Jerusalem, it was too dark to search. They went to the home of Joseph's cousin and told him what had happened. He welcomed them in: "Stay with us, and tomorrow you can look for the boy."

Mary and Joseph couldn't sleep, but they rose early and inquired among their acquaintances about any news of Jesus. No one had seen him. They searched the streets, but Jerusalem was still crowded with tens of thousands of visitors who had come for the Passover. Though the prospect of finding Jesus among all these people seemed dim, they pressed on. Finally, after two days Joseph suggested that they return to the Temple. "I know it's unlikely that we can find him in the crowds even if he is there," said Joseph, "but at least we can pray for God's assistance."

And so it was that after three days they found Jesus sitting among a group of teachers, listening to them and asking them questions. Mary and Joseph shouted with joy and ran quickly to embrace him. "Dear child," said Mary, "why have you done this? We have been searching anxiously for you for three days. We were afraid you were lost forever!" Neither she nor Joseph could understand his reply: "Why were you searching for me? Did you not know that I must be in my Father's house." After a few moments of silence, Mary smiled and said, "You are safe. That's all that matters. Let's go home."

Jesus bid a quick farewell to the teachers, took his mother's hand, and walked with her and Joseph from the Temple court. He would be obedient to them as he grew older and wiser. But Mary never forgot what he had said about his "Father's house." She treasured the words and the mystery they contained. He was like his Mother in many ways, but he would always be beyond her too. After all, that magnificent Temple was his home, wasn't it?

∽∘∾

Behind the finding in the Temple is Luke's wish to show the human and divine dimensions in Jesus, and the mystery implied there (John 1:14). The reference to the three days is perhaps a hint of the death and resurrection of Jesus; if so, this mystery is related to these events.

Luke again points to the faithfulness of Mary and Joseph to the law, for he mentions that they went to Jerusalem for the Passover every year. They were observing the laws found in Exodus 12 and Deuteronomy 16:1-8.

Luke 2:52, "And Jesus increased in wisdom and in years," is an invitation to reflect on the hidden years between his twelfth and thirtieth (Luke 3:23) birthdays. Chapter Nine offers background material for meditation on these years.

∽∘∾

The New Testament does not blame Joseph and Mary for losing Jesus. We, too, sometimes "lose" Jesus through no fault of our own. Our prayers seem to go nowhere and Christ seems to be absent. The fifth joyful mystery encourages us to keep seeking the Lord, as Mary and Joseph did, until he is found.

We may also "lose" Jesus because we do not put him first in our lives or because we sin. This mystery invites us to seek the Lord through repentance.

∽∘∾

Reflecting on the pain of Mary and Joseph can remind us to pray for parents who "lose" their children as runaways or as victims of abduction. We pray also for parents who "lose" their children spiritually because those children abandon God or the Church.

This mystery inspires us to pray for homeless children and for children waiting to be found through adoption. We ask God's blessings on adoptive and foster parents, and on those who care for children and adolescents separated from their families.

Mary's inability to understand Jesus' remarks in the Temple is paralleled by the experience of many parents as their children grow up and gradually leave the nest. There are the inevitable misunderstandings, arguments, and silences as children become adolescents and struggle with the issues of identity and self-worth. We pray for parents and children, that they may have the joy of finding one another.

THE BIBLE TRANSLATED INTO PRAYER

The rosary is "the Bible translated into prayer," then into the book of our lives. For almost a thousand years, Catholics have entered into the mysteries of the Bible through the rosary. We have seen how the joys of Mary and Jesus can touch our lives and the lives of those for whom we pray. Now we turn to their sorrows.

Questions for Discussion and Reflection

When you pray the rosary, how do you meditate on the mysteries? Are you familiar with other ways of meditating while praying the rosary, such as the Scriptural Rosary, where a verse from the New Testament is read before each Hail Mary?

Have you ever thought of the rosary as "the Bible translated into prayer"? Do you agree that this is a good description of the rosary? Why or why not?

Rosary means "rose garden." Have you ever considered the rosary as a gift of flowers, a bouquet of prayers, to your Mother Mary?

Some people criticize Catholics for praying the rosary because they say that Jesus forbids repetition in prayer in Matthew 6:7-8. How would you answer this criticism? (Note: One possible answer is given below in the Activities. But try to develop your own response before looking!)

Activities

Consider this response to the criticism that the rosary is repetitive prayer forbidden by Jesus:

In Matthew 6:7-8, Jesus does not say that we should not repeat prayers. Jesus says: "When you are praying, do not heap up empty phrases as the Gentiles do, for they think that they will be heard because of their many words." Jesus does say that we should not heap up empty phrases as do the Gentiles, who were pagans. Pagan prayer is not just praying the same prayer often; pagan prayer is supposing that God owes us something for each word we utter. Pagan prayer is bargaining with God. Jesus does not mean that we must not repeat prayers; if he did, we could say the Lord's Prayer only once in our lifetime. The Bible itself contains repetitious prayers; see, for example, Psalm 136, which repeats the phrase "for his steadfast love endures forever" twenty-six times. Jesus repeated prayers: see Matthew 26:39,42,44. Jesus "prayed for the third time, saying the same words" (Matthew 26:44).

When we pray the words of the rosary, we are not bargaining with God. We are calming our bodies and focusing our minds so that we can meditate on the mysteries of our faith. The rosary is one of the best Christian prayers precisely because it helps us concentrate on the truths taught in the Bible.

Try to add your own reasons to this explanation and "Always be ready to make your defense to anyone who demands from you an accounting for the hope that is in you" (1 Peter 3:15).

CHAPTER 11

MARY'S ROSARY:
THE SORROWFUL
MYSTERIES

Michelle was only eight years old, but she had endured many surgeries to repair serious birth defects. I visited her often at the hospital and in her home, and never left without a sense of awe at her patience and cheerfulness. She loved Jesus and believed that she would one day be with him.

The time came when the doctors could do no more for Michelle. She knew that she was dying, and she faced death without fear. At her funeral, certain that we were honoring a saint, I told her family and the congregation that Michelle brought Colossians 1:24 to life: "I am now rejoicing in my sufferings for your sake, and in my flesh I am completing what is lacking in Christ's afflictions for the sake of his body, that is, the church."

What could be lacking? Perhaps saints like Michelle to bring the reality of Christ's saving death into the here and now. Michelle, a little child, showed that heroic endurance of pain, without complaint, without bitterness, always with love and often with a smile, is possible. She was a living sign of the love of Christ, who accepted suffering and death for our sake.

HUMAN SUFFERING AND BELIEF IN GOD

"How can anyone believe in a God who allows so much suffering, especially in innocent children?" Some may deny God's existence because they cannot understand the suffering of little children, but the children themselves seem to be brought into God's loving arms by their pain. I have visited children who were suffering so much that I had to leave the room choking back tears. But I have never seen their faith shaken by the pain they endured. To them, Jesus was a friend, more real than their pain.

Ryan, four years old, was diagnosed with cancer. He underwent surgery. Afterward, doctors told his parents that chemotherapy would be necessary. The evening before it was to begin, his mother explained the procedure and told Ryan that his hair would fall out. "I know," he said, "Jesus told me it would."

Sue, a nurse who worked with terminally ill children, said that it was painful to see her patients suffer so much. "But," she said, "their faith and their down-to-earth relationship with God have strengthened my faith. Those little children see Jesus!"

Doctor Diane M. Komp, a pediatrician who cares for many critically ill children, writes that she abandoned her religious beliefs during medical training. She could not reconcile suffering with the existence of a loving God. Then she had a number of startling experiences involving young children near death. They saw Jesus and were comforted by God's grace. Gradually, she says, their simple, unclouded trust in God restored her own faith. She learned also from the parents. Some understandably grew angry with God at the death of their children. But they did not lose their faith. "I found," Doctor Komp writes, "that those who walk through the valley of the shadow of death do not walk alone. God becomes a cosufferer" (*Guideposts*, August 1992).

THE PASSION OF JESUS AND OUR PAIN

If there were an easy answer to the problem of pain, Jesus would have given it. Instead, he immersed himself in our suffering. He became a cosufferer with us.

Saint Paul accepted hunger, thirst, beatings, stonings, and imprisonment. In these sufferings, he felt Jesus enter his very being. "I have been crucified with Christ," he wrote, "and it is no longer I who live, but it is Christ who lives in me" (Galatians 2:19-20). His experience has been repeated in the lives of saints for two thousand years, canonized saints like Francis of Assisi and saints like Michelle.

THE SORROWS OF MARY AND OUR GRIEF

Mary, too, is a cosufferer. She stood at the cross of Jesus and shared in his agony. She held the broken body of her son in her arms. She now stands near parents who wait at the bedside of suffering children. She embraces those who mourn the death of a child.

She is also a consoler. Her presence at the cross was a consolation to Jesus as he was ridiculed by the people he had come to save. Her presence at Joseph's deathbed brought him comfort and peace as he breathed his last. She has ministered to the suffering and dying for two thousand years. Out of this fact, experienced by innumerable Christians, has come the prayer, "Holy Mary, Mother of God, pray for us sinners, now and at the hour of our death."

MYSTERY INTO LIFE: THE SORROWFUL MYSTERIES

The mystery of Christ's presence in those who suffer does not eliminate their pain, nor does it explain why innocent people endure affliction. But his presence is real, and somehow we must translate the mystery into life. One proven way of doing this is praying the Sorrowful Mysteries of the rosary. These mysteries place before us the awful agonies that Jesus accepted for our sake. The rosary gives us time to let their reality sink in. It gives us time to consider the suffering we face and to unite it to the passion of Christ. It gives us time to become aware of the suffering endured by countless millions on this earth and to place these people in Christ's care.

The rosary also reminds us of the sorrows Mary experienced and of her maternal love for all human beings. The rosary allows us to stand with Mary beneath the cross of Jesus as he says, "Here is your mother." The rosary assures us that we are never alone in our suffering. If we are on the cross of pain, we are crucified with Christ, and standing near the cross is Mary.

The Sorrowful Mysteries of the rosary can help us face and conquer the suffering that is an inevitable part of life. One of my hopes is that through the rosary I will receive the grace to handle suffering as well as some of the great believers I have known. My Aunt Corinne spent her last eight years in a nursing home. In all the years I visited her, I never saw her without her rosary. I never heard her complain. She always had a smile and seemed more concerned about others than about herself.

Anna, in her eighties, was paralyzed by a stroke and had control only of her right hand and arm. She lay in bed for nine years, praying the rosary. Only God knows how many people were helped by the thousands of times she prayed her beads.

Like Anna and Corinne, we, too, find strength in the Sorrowful Mysteries of the rosary. Like them, we can learn that suffering and death are not an end, but a doorway to new life. Like them, we can join our sufferings to Christ's for the good of others.

Like them, we can say with Saint Paul: "I want to know Christ and the power of his resurrection and the sharing of his sufferings by becoming like him in his death, if somehow I may attain the resurrection from the dead" (Philippians 3:10-11).

THE FIRST SORROWFUL MYSTERY— THE AGONY IN THE GARDEN
Matthew 26:36-56; Mark 14:32-51; Luke 22:39-53

Jesus and his disciples left Jerusalem and walked northeast through the Kidron Valley to a garden called Gethsemane on the Mount of Olives. At the entrance of the garden, he turned toward them. Even in the dim light of evening, they could see the sorrow and fear in his eyes. "Sit here while I pray," he said. "Peter, James, John, please come too. All of you, pray that you may not give in to temptation and trial." He walked further into the garden, then asked Peter, James, and John to wait under an olive tree. They watched him go a few steps more, throw himself on the ground, and call out, "Abba, Father, if it is possible, let this cup of pain pass from me. But may your will, not mine, be done." As his prayers continued, the apostles, one by one, fell asleep.

"I'm sorry, Lord," mumbled Peter. "We are just so tired. We'll try to stay awake. I promise." Jesus looked sadly at him, then at the others. They were good men, though weak. But how could he go on alone? He went back and prayed in the same words. Sweat, then blood, began running down his face. Almost overwhelmed with grief and fear, he suddenly felt a presence, an angel of light. Resolution and determination returned, and he said again and again, "Father, your will be done. Your will be done."

But he wanted human companionship too, the assurance that his friends would be with him. He shook them awake. "I understand," he said. "I know you are trying, but you are tired and weak. All the more reason to pray."

Again he prayed, and again he felt strength flow into his body and spirit. "Father, if this cup of suffering must be drained, then I will take it from your hands." Suddenly, at the gate of the garden, Jesus saw the flare of lanterns and the glint of swords. "Get up," he said to the apostles. "My betrayer is here." A group of soldiers moved swiftly through the gates, led by a man who walked past the apostles and went directly to Jesus. He put his arms on Jesus' shoulders, then kissed him.

Soldiers moved in and held Jesus' arms behind him. The apostles stood near, shouting and gesturing. Suddenly a sword flashed and a man shrieked with pain. "No, Peter," commanded Jesus. "If I wanted war, God would send legions of angels." Confused and frightened, Peter and the other apostles turned and ran, leaving Jesus at the mercy of his foes.

ᴖᴖᴖ

Several other New Testament passages reflect Christ's agony in the garden. Hebrews 5:7 says, "Jesus offered up prayers and supplications, with loud cries and tears, to the one who was able to save him from death, and he was heard because of his reverent submission." John 12:20-36 has many of the same elements as the garden scene, including Jesus' anguish and a sign of comfort from heaven. The accounts of the Last Supper are also appropriate material for reflection during this mystery.

Old Testament background includes the experience of Adam and Eve in the garden of Eden (Genesis 3). Their disobedience was remedied by the obedience of Jesus in the garden of Gethsemane.

∽∘∾

We can relate the agony to our own lives in a number of ways. When we are faced with suffering or pain, we can turn to Jesus for strength. Jesus was betrayed by one of his followers and abandoned by the rest. We are one with him when we are betrayed by false friends. Jesus was faithful to God's will, even when he was not appreciated or supported by others. Parents whose children fail to show appreciation, as well as anyone whose efforts are "taken for granted," can turn to Jesus in the garden for strength.

We should remember, too, that the failure of his disciples to support Jesus in his agony must have been one of his most painful burdens. Christ must have thought about all he had come to save. He must have been weighed down by the sins of future generations. If Jesus had seen our lives, would they have been a consolation to him?

∽∘∾

This mystery should lead us to pray for all members of Christ's body who are experiencing anguish and distress. People diagnosed with a serious illness, anyone struggling with mental or emotional sickness, and those disheartened by failure share in some way in the agony of Christ. We can pray for them and seek consolation for them. Our own experiences of being unappreciated can remind us of others in the same situation. We place them in Christ's care.

THE SECOND SORROWFUL MYSTERY— THE SCOURGING AT THE PILLAR

Matthew 27:26; Mark 15:15; Luke 23:16,22; John 19:1

After his arrest in the garden, Jesus was taken before the Jewish court, the Sanhedrin. He was interrogated by Caiaphas, the high priest, and by Annas, father-in-law of Caiaphas. The court ruled that Jesus was guilty of blasphemy and ought to be put to death. After the decision, those who hated him because he had attacked their business dealings in the Temple and those who detested his religious views had him at their mercy. Jesus was blindfold, ridiculed, and beaten. In the morning, the leaders assembled. They wished to avoid the blame for Jesus' death, and they wanted him to suffer the humiliation of a Roman crucifixion. So they took him to the Roman procurator, Pontius Pilate, who was residing at the Fortress Antonia, near the Temple complex. Pilate questioned Jesus and decided that he was innocent. After learning that Jesus was a Galilean, Pilate sent him to Herod Antipas, in Jerusalem for the Passover. Herod had long wanted to see Jesus, but when Jesus refused to answer his questions, Herod mocked Jesus and sent him back to Pilate. According to Luke and John, at this point Pilate had Jesus scourged to placate the Jewish leaders. Matthew and Mark mention the scourging as part of a death sentence issued by Pilate.

None of the gospels describes the scourging in detail, perhaps because a Roman scourging was too horrible to dwell on. Those sentenced to scourging were stripped, tied to a low pillar, then beaten by two soldiers with heavy whips made of many leather thongs containing jagged pieces of metal and bone. The leather, metal, and bone ripped through skin, muscle, and tendons, leaving the victim's flesh hanging in tatters. Such a scourging caused unimaginable pain, and often brought its victim to the point of death.

Two soldiers tied Jesus to a low post. "Now, King of the Jews," one of them taunted, "we are going to beat you bloody." Jesus said nothing, but he could feel his knees trembling with dread. A whistling sound tore the air and ended in the slap and crunch of leather, metal, and bone against flesh. Jesus gasped with pain. A second blow brought him to his knees. Blow upon blow rained down until Jesus felt that his entire body had been shredded. Blood ran everywhere, and bits of his flesh fell to the ground. "Abba, Father," Jesus moaned, and he fell awkwardly on his side. "Stop," a command rang out. "Don't kill the poor fool…yet!"

∽∞∽

New Testament background for the scourging includes the gospel accounts of the events between Jesus' arrest and the scourging. These are summarized above and may be found in Matthew 26:57-27:25; Mark 14:53-15:14; Luke 22:54-23:25; John 18:12-40.

Isaiah 53 portrayed Israel as a servant whose suffering would bring redemption to the nations. In this and in other Suffering Servant passages, Isaiah foreshadowed a deeper reality, the salvation given to the world through the passion and death of Christ. Isaiah 53 can be read as background for all the Sorrowful Mysteries.

∽∾∾

The scourging inflicted terrible physical pain on Jesus. Meditation on this mystery is an opportunity to consider how we handle the pain that comes our way. Do we complain and give in to self-pity, thus making ourselves and others more miserable? Or do we try to bear unavoidable sufferings bravely by offering "our bodies as a living sacrifice, holy and acceptable to God"? (Romans 12:1) Do we accept everyday aches and discomforts with equanimity and a sense of humor? Do we join our sufferings, great and small, to those of Christ for the sake of his Body, the Church?

∽∾∾

The physical suffering of Jesus continues in his body on earth. As we meditate on Christ's scourging, we can pray for all who are persecuted and tortured because of their faith in Christ. We pray for people, especially friends, relatives, and acquaintances, who must endure pain from disease, injury, or chronic illness. We pray for victims of physical abuse, crime, and war. Remembering that Jesus must have suffered terribly from thirst and hunger as his ordeal dragged on, we pray for those who lack food and water.

THE THIRD SORROWFUL MYSTERY— THE CROWNING WITH THORNS

Matthew 27:27-30; Mark 15:16-20; John 19:2-5

"O King of the Jews," the huge Syrian mercenary sneered, "we are sorry if we hurt you. Now we want to make you feel better. Look, we brought you a crown and a nice royal robe!" His companions roared with laughter. They forced Jesus onto an old bench, and each walked up, made a mock genuflection, then stood close around him. The Syrian held a filthy red cloak, and on the cloak a crown fashioned from long, sharp thorns. "First your crown, O King," he shouted, and nodded to his companions. One of them picked up the crown with his sword, laid it on Jesus' head, then pressed it into his scalp with the flat of the sword. "And now your royal robe," the big soldier laughed. He slapped the cloak on Jesus' shoulders, looked for a moment with contempt at him, then jeered, "How about some tribute, O mighty King!" He spat in Jesus' face and then took a long, heavy reed from the woodpile and placed it in Jesus' hand. "Your scepter, Sire," he mocked. The reed fell to the ground. The soldier picked it up and whipped it against the crown of thorns. Blood ran down Jesus' forehead into his eyes and mouth. Another soldier snatched the reed and pounded the crown of thorns while the others, dancing around Jesus with glee, spat into his face. Until they were exhausted by their own hatred, they poured out on Jesus their contempt for Jews and their frustration at being stationed in that hostile land.

Jesus shows in this mystery that he lived what he taught. He accepted humiliation for our sake and by his conduct reinforced his words in Luke 18:14: "All who humble themselves will be exalted." Acts 8:32-33 quotes Isaiah 53 in reference to Jesus' humiliation. The First Letter of Peter (2:20-25) recalls the abuse and sufferings Christ endured and challenges us to imitate his courage and humility.

As Christ was treated unfairly, so, too, at times are we. This does not mean that we must let people walk over us with impunity. There are times to speak up and times to be silent. Jesus did not "turn the other cheek" when he was struck by one of the temple police (John 18:22-23). This man was a Jew, and Jesus knew that a reprimand might help him see the error of his ways. But when Christ found himself at the mercy of the Roman soldiers, he knew that any resistance was useless and would only feed their rage. So he took their ridicule with dignity and silence. When speaking in our own defense can help us or others, we should speak. At other times, we are called to imitate the quiet courage of Christ.

‿oo‿

Humiliation and degradation can be harder to bear than physical suffering. This mystery opens our eyes to victims of persecution who are stripped of their dignity and treated like animals. Christ is crowned with thorns and mocked anew when an innocent person is falsely accused, when a child is ridiculed on the playground, when a teenager is excluded by peers or made fun of, when anyone is subjected to emotional abuse. As we pray this mystery, we place all these hurt and frightened people in the care of Christ, who knows the pain of being mocked and scorned.

THE FOURTH SORROWFUL MYSTERY— JESUS CARRIES THE CROSS

Matthew 27:31-34; Mark 15:20-24; Luke 23:26-32; John 19:17

Pilate looked with disgust at the mob clamoring for the death of Jesus. "All right," he shouted. "Let him be crucified, and let his blood be on your heads!" To the centurion standing at his right he gave the order, "Take him and crucify him."

"O King," leered the mercenary, "guess what? We are going to nail you to your throne. But first we have to dress you in your own clothes so everyone can recognize you and pay you homage." With that he ripped the red cloak from Jesus, re-opening the wounds of the scourging. He and another soldier clothed Jesus in his own robe. Then they took a heavy, wooden beam and laid it on Christ's shoulders. "Your throne, King," laughed the mercenary, "but you'll have to carry it to your palace." A soldier took a rope and tied it loosely around Jesus' neck, then led him outside the fortress toward Golgotha, a hill about a third of a mile west of the city walls.

Jesus, staggering under the weight of the beam and weakened by loss of blood, kept stumbling on the rough pavement. Several times he fell heavily, only to be beaten until he struggled up again. Finally, he collapsed, unable to rise. The centurion intervened. "Stop hitting him," he commanded, "or he'll die here." He turned to a bystander. "What is your name?" "Simon, from Cyrene, in Africa," replied the big man. "Well, Simon, pick up his cross and follow him, or we'll crucify you too." Simon lifted up the cross and carried it behind Jesus as he was dragged on by the soldiers.

By now word had spread that Jesus was being led to crucifixion. A group of women stood on the roadside just outside the city gates, waiting for him to pass. Some were crying. Jesus paused and looked at them with gratitude and pity. "Daughters of Jerusalem," Jesus said, "I know you care, and I am grateful. But don't weep for me. Weep for yourselves and your children. For terrible things will come upon this city."

All too soon they arrived at the barren hill of Golgotha. Three tall posts had been planted in the rocky ground, and the soldiers halted before the one in the center. Seizing the crossbeam from Simon, they dropped it onto the ground. They took off Jesus' robe, opening his wounds yet again, and threw him down on top of the crossbeam. Soldiers grasped his arms and stretched them along the beam. They drove heavy nails through his wrists, fastening him to the wood. Jesus moaned with pain as the nails ripped through flesh and bone. He cried out in agony as the soldiers stood up with the beam and lifted it atop the center post, suspending Jesus just above the ground. The mercenary nailed his feet to the post, then stood back and jeered, "Well, King, how do you like your throne?"

∽∞∾

The New Testament tells us that we must deny ourselves, take up the cross daily, and follow Jesus (Luke 9:23; Matthew 16:24; Mark 8:34). This powerful image sees us as followers of Jesus, picking up the cross as Jesus did, and walking in his footsteps on the way to Golgotha.

Early Church teachers interpreted Abraham's readiness to offer his son Isaac as a foreshadowing of Christ's Passion (Genesis 22). Isaac carried the wood for his own sacrifice, as Christ would later carry the wood of the cross.

∽∞∾

Luke 9:23 is an application of the Passion of Christ to our

life. This passage teaches us to imitate the self-denial and sacrificial love of Christ as we take up the cross daily. We do this when we accept inconveniences cheerfully, fulfill our obligations and duties in spite of weariness, and offer up pain and emotional suffering.

The fourth sorrowful mystery teaches perseverance. Christ struggled on in spite of dreadful pain, hunger, thirst, and fatigue. We imitate him when we remain faithful, no matter what the cost, even when we seem to be alone.

Simon of Cyrene carried the cross of Christ. We imitate him every time we shoulder someone's burden, whether in small matters like taking out the trash or in great matters like being a big brother or big sister to a troubled child.

There are people everywhere who carry a cross. For some, it is the cross of physical pain, sickness, amputation of limbs, paralysis, old age. For others, there are crosses like failing in school; not making a team; losing a job; failing in business; being victimized by disasters like floods, fires, and storms. The fourth sorrowful mystery gives us occasion to think about all who struggle under a cross, and to pray for them.

THE FIFTH SORROWFUL MYSTERY— THE CRUCIFIXION

Matthew 27:33-66; Mark 15:24-47; Luke 23:32-56; John 19:18-42

On the cross Jesus suffered the horrors of crucifixion. The nails from which he was suspended had pierced flesh, nerves, and bone. Fiery pain shot from his arms and legs throughout his frame. The weight of his body caused him to sink down until cramping and constriction of chest muscles started to suffocate him. He then pulled himself up on the nails, which grated against bone and flesh, in order to breathe. When he again became too weak to stand the pain of the nails, he sank down until the awful need for air forced him upward. For hours, in waves of unspeakable torment, Jesus endured his crucifixion.

After suspending Jesus from his cross, the soldiers went about the business of crucifying two criminals. Then they took a sign Pilate had sent and nailed it to the top of Jesus' cross. The sign read: "Jesus of Nazareth, King of the Jews." "Well, King Jesus," said one of the soldiers, "now everybody will recognize you." "The king won't be using his cloak," another shouted. "It's a little bloody, but otherwise in good shape. Let's roll dice for it."

Some of Jesus' enemies had come out to witness the spectacle. "Aha, Jesus," they shouted, "if you are God's son, come on down from the cross!" The two criminals, mad with pain, joined in the mockery. One grew quiet, however, when he heard Jesus pray, "Father, forgive them. They do not know what they are doing." "Are you insane?" screamed the criminal on Jesus' left. "If you are the Messiah, kill them all! Save yourself, and us." Then the criminal on Jesus' right shouted, "Aren't you afraid even of God? We're getting what we deserve, but Jesus has done nothing wrong." A moment of silence followed. Then he turned his head toward Jesus and looked into his eyes. "Jesus," he said, "I'm sorry for what I've done. Remember me when you come into your kingdom." "Today," Jesus replied, "you will be with me in heaven." In spite of his pain, the criminal smiled. "Yes," he said, "I believe it. I believe it."

Standing at a distance were a few followers of Jesus. Weeping and praying, they held one another for comfort. A woman emerged from the group, with a young man at her side. They walked toward the cross in the center. The soldiers looked up from their dice game. The centurion, who had followed the procession to Golgotha and had been standing off to the side, started to draw his sword. But something in the eyes of the woman made him pause. He sheathed the sword and said to his soldiers, "Move back. We'll stand guard over here."

The woman walked to the cross of Jesus and gently touched him. Tears streamed down her face. The young man placed his arm around her. Jesus looked at them silently for a long time, then said, "Woman, here is your son. Here is your mother."

Suddenly the sky grew dark. The wind picked up and black clouds formed overhead. A bolt of lightning struck not far from Golgotha. Jesus looked toward the sky, strained upward, and cried out, "My God, my God, why have you forsaken me?"

The pain seemed to consume his whole being. With blood draining from his body, unbearable thirst parched his mouth and throat, and he moaned, "I am thirsty." The centurion took a sponge and soaked it in sour wine he had brought. He held it to Jesus' lips, but Jesus seemed too weak to drink it.

Another bolt of lightning tore the sky open. Rain fell in torrents and bystanders scattered for cover. Cold gusts of wind roared down from the north. The soldiers, frightened at the violence of the storm, looked at the centurion, but he said nothing. He was watching Jesus, whose face now was luminous with a look of peace, almost of joy. "It is finished," Jesus cried out. "Father, into your hands I commend my spirit!"

There was silence. The rain stopped as suddenly as it had begun. Jesus' Mother began to sob. The centurion walked over to her, took her hand, and said, "Truly, this man was the Son of God!"

❧

New Testament passages related to the Crucifixion include Jesus' predictions of his Passion (Luke 9:21-22), the meditation on Christ's death found in John 3:13-18, and Paul's hymn in Philippians 2:6-11 on the humiliation and exaltation of Jesus. Colossians 1:24, Galatians 2:19-20, and Philippians 3:10, quoted earlier in this chapter, will help us integrate this mystery into our own lives.

John 3:14-15 compares Christ's being raised up on the cross to an Old Testament incident in Numbers 21:4-9. When the Israelites were attacked during the Exodus by poisonous snakes, Moses fashioned a bronze serpent and put it on a pole. Those who looked with faith at this sign of God's protection were healed.

When Jesus called out, "My God, my God, why have you forsaken me?" he was quoting Psalm 22. The entire Psalm foreshadows the Passion of Jesus, and the evangelists apparently had Psalm 22 in mind when they wrote the gospels.

❧

The death of Christ on the cross should alert us to our own mortality. We will certainly die, and the fifth sorrowful mystery gives us the opportunity to reflect on this reality. We should pray that Mary will be at our side at the moment of our death, just as she was near the cross of her son.

Like Saint Paul, we should unite our sufferings to those of Christ for the sake of the Church. We are then "crucified with Christ," and Christ lives in us. We are never closer to Jesus than when we are one with him in his sufferings.

This mystery is one of love, the love of Jesus—"No one has greater love than this, to lay down one's life for one's friends" (John 15:13)—and the love of Mary (see the reflections on love in Chapter Eight).

∽∘∾

As we pray the fifth sorrowful mystery, we should be especially attentive to the dying. We may know someone who has a terminal illness or someone near death because of old age. At any moment, many throughout the world are drawing their last breath. We pray for them.

Jesus forgave his enemies. Many people hurt by others carry the burden of revenge and resentment because they are unable to forgive. We pray that they may find in Christ's example the ability to forgive their enemies and so find peace of heart.

DEATH LEADS TO GLORY

If Christ's death had ended the story of his life, there would be no gospel, no Good News. But death leads to glory, glory so great that even the terrible sufferings of Christ were overcome. "I consider that the sufferings of this present time are not worth comparing with the glory about to be revealed to us" (Romans 8:18). And so the Sorrowful Mysteries of the rosary lead to the Glorious.

Questions for Discussion and Reflection

Are you familiar with the Stations of the Cross? Which of the stations were referred to in the meditations above? Which were not? Do you think that considering the Stations while praying the fourth and fifth mysteries might be a good way to meditate on the rosary?

Had you realized that Christ died of asphyxiation? (Of course, loss of blood and physical trauma also contributed to his death.) John says that the Jewish leaders did not want the three bodies left on the cross at Golgotha during the sabbath. So to hasten the death of the two criminals, the soldiers broke their legs. Why would breaking their legs hasten their death?

Christ was already dead when the soldiers broke the legs of the other two. So a soldier put a lance into his side to guarantee the fact of his death. John remarks that blood and water poured from Christ's side. In John's theology, blood and water symbolize the Eucharist and baptism. What connection do you think John was making between Christ's death and these sacraments?

Activities

Pray a "newspaper rosary." Scan the headlines of a newspaper and note those who are suffering in any way. There are victims of crime, war, accidents, natural disasters. There are the sick and troubled. There are the deceased and their sorrowing families. After noting these people, at least in a general way, put aside the paper and pray the Sorrowful Mysteries of the rosary for them. As you do, picture Mary standing near each suffering individual, offering strength and consolation.

Slowly and reflectively say the following prayer.

Memorare

Remember, O most gracious Virgin Mary, that never was it known that anyone who fled to your protection, implored your help, or sought your intercession was left unaided. Inspired with this confidence, I fly to you, O virgin of virgins, my Mother.

To you I come, before you I stand, sinful and sorrowful. O Mother of the Word Incarnate, despise not my petitions, but in your mercy, hear and answer me. Amen.

CHAPTER

12

MARY'S ROSARY: THE GLORIOUS MYSTERIES

When Tom was seven years old, he was visiting friends at a farm. He walked behind a fractious horse and was kicked in the head. Near death from a skull fracture, he was rushed to a hospital. Doctors worked frantically to repair damage and ease the pressure on his brain. At one point, Tom stopped breathing, but was revived by the medical team. After a week in the hospital, he was well enough to return home, where he completely recovered.

While on the operating table, Tom had a "near-death" experience. He felt himself leaving his physical body. In a new body, he walked through a meadow toward a brook that was crossed by a bridge. On the bridge was a beautiful woman he somehow knew was Mary, the Mother of Jesus. She assured Tom that he would not die, and that he would return to his family.

Thirty years later, Tom told me that the experience seemed as real as the day it happened. He was certain of life after death, and he was not afraid to die because he knew that Mary and Jesus would bring him to eternal life. Tom's experience proved to him that Mary was a Mother who watched over him, in life and in death.

This is not surprising, because Mary was present at the moment of Christ's death. She was present when he passed from this mortal life to eternity. The Glorious Mysteries honor Mary as someone intimately connected with the miracle of Christ's Resurrection and with Christ's promise of eternal life for us.

THE GLORIOUS MYSTERIES: THE OTHER SIDE OF DEATH

After Jesus was taken from the cross, friends hastily arranged his burial before the Jewish sabbath rest began. A Roman guard was posted at his tomb.

On the third day after his death, some women followers went to the burial place to anoint his body. Astonished to find the stone rolled back and the tomb empty, they ran to tell his apostles. No one knew what to make of the empty tomb until Jesus appeared, risen and glorious.

Because the followers of Jesus first saw him on Easter Sunday, they spoke of him as rising on the third day. Hearing this, we may suppose that Christ lay dead in the tomb from Friday afternoon until Sunday morning. That, however, could not have been the case because Christ is God. It is true that his physical body was placed in a tomb, but he continued to live in what Saint Paul calls a "spiritual body" (1 Corinthians 15:44). The Bible affirms this, for before he died, Jesus said to one of the criminals crucified with him, "Today you will be with me in Paradise" (Luke 23:43).

After Christ's mortal body was buried, it did not decay. Instead, it was glorified, taking on the qualities of a "spiritual body," and was reunited to the person of Christ. We do not know exactly when this happened, but it may well have been on Easter Sunday morning.

Because Christ is God as well as human, he was able to come back from the other side of death as he pleased. He allowed himself to be seen, heard, and touched by his followers.

This ought not make us think that Christ's Resurrection was like the raising of Lazarus (John 11:1-44). Lazarus came back to our world of sickness and death, and the last thing he ever did on earth was die again! Christ, by contrast, conquered death itself. He did not return to our mortal existence. He passed through death to eternal life. If a Roman soldier had tried to kill the risen Jesus by plunging a sword into him, the sword could have done Christ no harm. "We know that Christ, being raised from the dead, will never die again; death no longer has dominion over him" (Romans 6:9).

There is a mystery here. Once Christ passed through death, he progressed beyond the reach of scientific instruments and historical observation. The descriptions of his appearances in the four gospels are essentially efforts to put into words wonders which transcend time and space.

Christ's Resurrection and the other Glorious Mysteries are miraculous and mysterious. But they are real. The apostles were so sure of the reality of the Resurrection that they gladly gave their lives for Christ. We may find it hard to understand the Resurrection and the other Glorious Mysteries, but they are as certain as the circling of the earth around the sun.

We meditate on them as facts, as realities, but also as miracles which surpass our human limitations. Words fail us. As we ponder the Glorious Mysteries of the rosary, we should do so with a sense of awe. "What no eye has seen, nor ear heard, / nor the human heart conceived, / what God has prepared for those who love him— / these things God has revealed to us through the Spirit" (1 Corinthians 2:9-10). These are the things we consider as we pray the Glorious Mysteries!

THE FIRST GLORIOUS MYSTERY— THE RESURRECTION

Matthew 28:1-15; Mark 16:1-18; Luke 24:1-49; John 20-21

Mary held the broken body of Christ in her arms for a long time. "I remember," she whispered, "the first time I held you. I thought my heart would burst with happiness. When you were small and something frightened you, you would come running to me. I remember when you left home to begin preaching. I held you for a long time before we said good-bye. And now, I know you hear me, Jesus. And I love you."

Nicodemus and Joseph gently took Jesus' body from her arms, and John led her to the home in Jerusalem where she had been staying. She closed the door and wept a long time. She prayed Psalm 23 again and again. On the sabbath she remained in her room. John visited her about noon. She was touched by his concern, and by his faith. "Jesus told us," John said, "that he would be crucified, and that he would rise on the third day. I believe in life after death, as Judas Maccabeus did. But I don't understand what Jesus meant. Mother, will we see him again here or only when we die?" Mary smiled gently when John called her "Mother." "Son," she replied, "that is in God's hands. I know, as you do, that he lives."

Early on the morning after the Sabbath, Mary rose and knelt in the dim light to pray. Tears flowed down her cheeks as once again she thought of all that Jesus had endured. Then she felt a hand on her shoulder. The room filled with light. "Jesus," she murmured, "Jesus. The Mighty One has done great things for me!"

The Bible does not say that Jesus appeared to Mary. But he certainly must have visited her, and we can meditate with much profit on the tenderness, love, and joy he shared with his Mother. As we meditate, we can ask Mary to help us experience the presence of the risen Jesus, who comes to us in the Eucharist and other sacraments, and who dwells in our hearts.

The first glorious mystery affords us an opportunity to meditate on Jesus' appearances to his apostles and other followers, as described in the gospels. Each appearance has significance for us. For example, the wonderful description of Jesus' appearance to the two disheartened disciples on the way to Emmaus teaches us to look for Jesus in the Scriptures and in the breaking of the bread (Luke 24:13-35).

೧౦౦

There are many passages related to the Resurrection of Jesus in the New Testament. Peter's first sermon on Pentecost proclaimed the Resurrection (Acts 2:22-36). It demonstrates a fact that should give us confidence in the reality of the Resurrection. The very apostles who had abandoned Jesus at his arrest witnessed to him fearlessly after his Resurrection. Though confronted by the same authorities who had earlier intimidated them, they preached that Jesus had risen. Their faith, and the faith of the early Church, was expressed by the apostle Thomas, who fell on his knees before Christ with the words, "My Lord and my God" (John 20:28).

Paul's great discourse in 1 Corinthians 15 on the Resurrection of Christ and the certainty of our own resurrection is a significant testimony to the belief of early Christians. "In fact Christ has been raised from the dead, the first fruits of those who have died" (1 Corinthians 15:20).

Peter's sermon on Pentecost and a later one by Paul (Acts 13:16-41) apply Psalm 16:7-11 to the Resurrection of Christ. The liturgy also interprets Psalm 110 in terms of the Resurrection. Passages in the Old Testament which affirm the reality of life after death, such as Wisdom 3:1-9 and 2 Maccabees 12:38-46, prepared the Israelites for belief in the Resurrection of Jesus.

✎

The first glorious mystery answers a question that every human being must ask: "What will happen to me when I die?" This mystery is an opportunity to reflect on our own death and to imagine the joy that will be ours when we share in the Resurrection of Christ. Then God will be with us and will wipe every tear from our eyes. Then "death will be no more; / mourning and crying and pain will be no more," and God will make all things new (Revelation 21:4-5).

John's Gospel connects the Resurrection to the forgiveness of sins. On Easter Sunday evening, Jesus appeared to the apostles, breathed the Holy Spirit upon them, and said, "If you forgive the sins of any, they are forgiven them" (John 20:19-23). Do we appreciate the sacrament of penance as Christ's special Easter gift to us? Do we use this sacrament to attain the peace Jesus offers by forgiving our sins?

John 6:51-58 connects the Eucharist and our resurrection to eternal life. We will live forever with the risen Christ if we put our faith in him and receive his body and blood in holy

Communion. Do we celebrate the Eucharist with faith and receive the Lord with devotion?

Romans 6:1-12 explains the link between the sacrament of baptism and Christ's death and resurrection. We must die to sin and live anew with Christ. The first glorious mystery asks if we are genuinely trying to overcome sin and to live in holiness.

∽∽

Meditation on the Resurrection of Christ should lead us to pray for all who have died, especially our loved ones. As we meditate on this mystery, we may picture those who die as walking into the loving arms of Christ, being greeted by Mary, the saints, family and friends.

The connection between the Resurrection of Jesus and the sacraments of baptism, penance, and Eucharist should prompt us to pray for those preparing to receive these sacraments.

THE SECOND GLORIOUS MYSTERY— THE ASCENSION

Matthew 28:16-20; Mark 16:19-20; Luke 24:50-53; Acts 1:1-11

Peter shuddered for a moment as he recalled the last time Jesus and the apostles had walked to the Mount of Olives...evening, the night before he died. But now it was day, a glorious spring day. The sun felt warm on his back. Birds were chirping in the olive trees. "It's hard to believe everything that has happened," thought Peter, "but it did."

Jesus turned toward Peter and the other apostles, smiled, and asked, "Peter, do you think you can be a rock of faith for my Church?" Peter smiled back, and answered, "Lord, I will try. You know how weak I am, but you know I love you." "Peter," said Jesus, "you will be a rock. I will send the Holy Spirit upon all of you. Stay in Jerusalem and pray until you are clothed with the Spirit's power." "How shall we know when this happens?" asked James. "You will know," said Jesus, "so will all the city."

They now stood near the top of Mount Olivet. "Go and make disciples of all nations," proclaimed Jesus solemnly. "Baptize them in the name of the Father, and of the Son, and of the Holy Spirit. You will not see me like this any longer. But I will be with you forever—in my word, in the sacred meal I gave you, in your love for one another." "You aren't leaving us, are you?" asked Philip. "We can do nothing without you." "I have come from the Father," Jesus explained. "And now I must go back. I am the first of all creation to return to the Father. But when I am lifted up from this earth, I will draw all people to myself, and I will make all things new."

What happened next was something none of the apostles could clearly explain. Jesus seemed to be raised upward, then gradually enveloped in a cloud until he vanished.

They stood there a long time. Then Thomas broke the silence. "Of course," he said. "A cloud. Just like the cloud of God's presence over our ancestors when they left Egypt! And he is now in heaven, with God, as God. He will be with us always because God is everywhere. No doubt about it. No doubt about it at all!"

∽∞∽

Closely related to the Ascension is Jesus' farewell address to his apostles found in John 14-17. These words are spoken to all who would follow Jesus until the end of time. They contain his promise to be with us forever, to send the Holy Spirit, to join us to himself in heaven.

Ephesians 1:17-23 reflects on the Resurrection, Ascension, and glorification of Jesus. See also Ephesians 4:7-16 and Colossians 3:1-17, passages which encourage us to look to Christ in heaven for the grace and inspiration to live a new life on earth. Hebrews 8:1-6 pictures Jesus at God's right hand as the high priest who leads us in worship.

The liturgy for Ascension Thursday interprets Psalms 47 and 68 as hymns of praise to Christ being lifted up to heaven.

∽∞∽

Christ promised to be with us always. His Ascension is a sign of his divinity and power. This decade of the rosary is a good time to ask ourselves if we remember Christ's presence in our hearts and in those around us. Do we read the Bible as his word? Do we worship him truly present in the Eucharist? Are we aware of his presence in the sacraments?

Christ told the apostles, and us, to make disciples of all nations. Do we try to evangelize by word and example? Jesus depends on us to show his love to others, to be his body, his heart and hands, on earth. Are we conscious of this, and do we try to "be Christ" to others?

∽○∼

The apostles traveled to many lands to make disciples and to baptize. This mystery of the rosary is an opportunity to pray for foreign missionaries and for those who preach the gospel. Many people have heard the gospel and are seeking the gift of faith. We pray that those who hear the Good News may believe and be baptized.

THE THIRD GLORIOUS MYSTERY— THE DESCENT OF THE HOLY SPIRIT
Acts 2:1-42

"Of course I believe in Jesus," said Bartholomew. "How could I not believe after what we've seen? But the idea of preaching the gospel to the whole world! Who will listen to us? We're just ordinary people, mostly fishermen." "And a former tax collector," added Matthew with a smile. "Yes, don't forget the tax collector," laughed Peter. "He is exhibit A. If Jesus could reform a Roman tax collector, anything is possible! Seriously, I'm a little frightened too. But Jesus said he would send the Holy Spirit, and that we would then do greater things than he did."

There was a lull in the conversation, then John turned to Mary. "Were you ever afraid?" "Yes, John," Mary replied. "I was very frightened when the angel first gave me God's message. I wondered how God could choose such an unimportant young woman from Nazareth. But God chooses the lowly to do great things. My advice is what it has always been: do whatever Jesus tells you, and he will overcome your fears."

"Well," said James, "we have been doing what Jesus asked. We've been waiting and praying for the Holy Spirit." "The Holy Spirit descended upon Jesus in the form of a dove," said Andrew. "I wonder how Jesus will send the Spirit to us. Let's pray again in the words Jesus taught us."

The group gathered together and prayed, "Our Father, who

art in heaven, hallowed be thy name. Thy kingdom come." Suddenly their prayer was drowned out by a roaring wind. The room shook. The dim light from the windows grew brighter until the very air seemed ablaze. Each one in the room felt a power like that of sails being filled by the wind. Each was touched with the fire of love and enlightenment. Instantly, what had seemed improbable now seemed certain. Yes, they would go into the whole world. And the world would never be the same.

Gradually, the wind died down and the light dimmed. There was perfect quiet in the room. And perfect peace. Then Peter said, "Let's go to the Temple. It is time to begin!"

∽∘∾

Acts 1:12-26 tells of the nine days the believers spent before the coming of the Holy Spirit. Mary, Mother of the Church, was with them as they waited and prayed. The remainder of the Acts of the Apostles describes the activity of the Holy Spirit in the Church. John 14:15-31 gives Jesus' promise to send the Holy Spirit. Romans 8 is a great testimony to the power of the Holy Spirit in the lives of believers. First Corinthians (12–13) describes the charismatic gifts of the Spirit experienced by the church at Corinth, then speaks of the greatest gift, love. Galatians 5:22-23 lists those effects of the Holy Spirit's indwelling known as the fruits of the Holy Spirit.

Peter, in his first Pentecost sermon, saw in Joel 3:1-5 (Joel 2:28-32 in some translations) a prophecy of the coming of the Holy Spirit. Isaiah 11:2 lists the qualities popularly called the gifts of the Holy Spirit.

∽∘∾

We have received the Holy Spirit, especially in baptism and confirmation. The third glorious mystery is a special time to examine our relationship to the Spirit. Are we aware that we are temples of the Holy Spirit (1 Corinthians 6:19)? Do we consciously nurture our friendship with the Holy Spirit? Are the gifts and the fruits of the Holy Spirit evident in our actions? Do we, prompted by the Holy Spirit, daily make the decision to love others as Jesus loves us? (See the reflections on Mary and the Holy Spirit in Chapter Eight.)

Each day we are faced with decisions, and need counsel and

guidance. We have tasks to perform, and need courage. This mystery is a time to pray for the assistance of the Holy Spirit.

❧

During the third glorious mystery, we can pray for the successors of the apostles, the bishops and our Holy Father. We pray for those in the RCIA who are waiting to receive the Holy Spirit in the sacraments of baptism and confirmation. We pray for young adults in confirmation preparation programs. We pray for students and their teachers, and for all who need the strength and guidance of the Holy Spirit in any way.

THE FOURTH GLORIOUS MYSTERY— THE ASSUMPTION OF MARY

1 Corinthians 15:20-26

The Bible, as was pointed out in Chapter Four, does not make explicit mention of Mary's Assumption. But the liturgy gives us 1 Corinthians 15:20-26 as the second reading for the Solemnity of the Assumption on August 15. The reading affirms that Christ has been raised from the dead, "the first fruits of those who have died." Just as all die in Adam, so all will rise in Christ, but each one in proper order. The liturgy thereby suggests that the proper order puts Mary, the Mother of Jesus, second after her son.

The Church's doctrine on the Assumption was explained in Chapter Four, and this mystery provides an opportunity to reflect on the Church's teaching and its meaning. But we should also try to imagine what Mary's last days on earth were like, and to picture that moment when she was reunited with her son in heaven.

"Mother, how are you feeling?" asked John. "Very tired," whispered Mary, with a weak smile. "I am sure that I will soon be going home. I am so happy to know that I will see Jesus face to face." "I know, Mother," said John, "but we will miss you. You are our closest link to Jesus." "Don't worry, John," Mary assured him. "I will be close to you and all the believers. And when Jesus calls you, I will be there at the hour of your death."

Then came a brief moment of darkness, which was quickly swept away by a light unlike any Mary had ever seen. She rose to find herself no longer in her little room, but at the outskirts of a great city. From within the city came the music of thousands of voices singing in harmony, "Holy, holy holy!" From the gate of the city walked a huge throng of people, their faces shining with an unearthly beauty and their garments bright as snow. Before them strode a King, her Lord and her God, her son. Mother and son embraced. There would be no more mourning, no more crying or pain. Her son had made all things new.

◆◆◆

Philippians 3:20-21 tells how Christ will make our bodies like his own. This has already happened to Mary through her Assumption, and she is Christ's pledge to us that our bodies, too, will be glorified. Ephesians 1:17-23 is a beautiful prayer that we may know the riches of our "glorious inheritance among the saints." Mary is first among those saints. In this mystery of the rosary, we ponder the glorious inheritance that is Mary's and that will one day be ours. First Thessalonians (4:16-17) relates Paul's concept of how we will be taken to heaven; it may be applied to Mary at her Assumption into heaven.

The first reading for the Vigil Mass of the Assumption is 1 Chronicles 15:3-4,15,16;16:1-2. These verses relate how David brought the Ark of the Covenant into Jerusalem. The liturgy sees the Ark as a symbol of Mary. The entry of the Ark into Jerusalem prefigures Mary's entry into heaven.

◆◆◆

This mystery is a reminder that we will one day die and stand before Jesus Christ, the just Judge (2 Timothy 4:8). Are we ready to meet the Lord now? Do we pray for a happy death? This mystery invites us to prepare, with hope and confidence in God's mercy, for the moment of our death.

◆◆◆

The fourth glorious mystery offers an opportunity to pray for the dying, and to ask Mary to be at the side of our loved ones at the moment of death. We ask Jesus to comfort the sick and dying through the sacrament of anointing of the sick.

The Assumption is yet another sign of the Church's belief that our bodies and material creation are good. Mary's body was not destroyed, but brought to glorified beauty and perfection. The Bible says that God gave the care of this earth over to us (Genesis 1:28). In some mysterious way, God's plan is that "creation itself will be set free from its bondage to decay and will obtain the freedom of the glory of the children of God" (Romans 8:21). We do not know how this will be accomplished, but we pray that people may work together to bring it about according to God's will. We pray that all may respect and care for the created things God has made. And, in company with Mary, "we wait for new heavens and a new earth, where righteousness is at home" (2 Peter 3:13).

THE FIFTH GLORIOUS MYSTERY—
THE CORONATION OF MARY
Revelation 11:19-12:17

"Thy kingdom come. Thy will be done on earth as in heaven." These words of the Lord's Prayer ask that God's kingdom may be fully established. Kings and queens are not as common as they were in Jesus' time, and "kingdom" symbolism may be hard to understand. But when we pray that God's kingdom might come, we are asking that all may know and do God's will, accept the salvation offered by Jesus Christ, and love God and others as Jesus does.

Jesus is "King of kings and Lord of lords" (Revelation 19:16). True peace and justice will come to our world only when all people recognize Christ's sovereignty. Unfortunately, too many human beings refuse to become part of God's kingdom, and the world suffers as a result. We are still a long way from doing God's will on earth as it is done in heaven.

Heaven is where we must look to find the perfection of the kingdom. There joy, peace, and love reign because all are in harmony with God's will and one with Jesus Christ. The saints in heaven are models for us, and because we are their brothers and sisters in Christ, they help us by their prayers. Among all the saints, Mary is first. She is honored as Queen because she is Mother of Christ the King, and because she has always been perfectly submissive to God's will and perfectly united with her son.

When we reflect on the fifth glorious mystery, we dream of how things ought to be on this earth, and how they are in heaven. We see Mary as the exemplar of what we hope to be. We turn to her as one who can help us achieve our dreams and our hopes.

Mary, you are the Mother of Jesus and the Queen of heaven. When God's temple in heaven is opened, we see you, the Ark of the Covenant. We honor you, the woman clothed with the sun, the moon under your feet, and on your head a crown of twelve stars.

You gave birth to a son, a male child, who rules all the nations. You are Mother of Christ. You have been taken up to heaven to a place prepared by God. You are our Queen, at the right hand of your son, the King of kings.

You are also the woman here on earth. You are Mother of the Church. You have shared the tribulations of all who have followed Jesus, and you have joined them in the war against Satan. You stood firm when hell did its worst against Jesus on the cross. You rejoiced when Jesus defeated death and hell by his Resurrection. You stand with those who keep the commandments of God and hold the testimony of Jesus so that after they share the cross of Christ they may also share his victory.

"Hail, holy Queen, Mother of mercy, our life, our sweetness, and our hope!"

❧

The Bible passages relevant to this mystery of the rosary have been explained in Chapter Three. The "queen mother" theme running through the Old and New Testaments can help us appreciate Mary's place of honor in heaven, and her motherly concern for us on earth.

❧

The fifth glorious mystery is a special time to contemplate our relationship to Mary. She is Queen and Mother to us now. We bring to her the cares and concerns of this day, knowing that she hears us and comes to our aid. We pray for the grace to hear Mary as she directs us to Jesus with the words, "Do whatever he tells you."

Mary as Queen should remind us of all who have won the victory and "reign forever and ever" with Christ (Revelation 22:5). Gathered around Mary are our loved ones who have gone before us. The fifth glorious mystery is a time to draw close to them and enjoy their company, for they care for us and pray for us as Mary does.

∾

During this mystery we can place in Mary's care all those we know who need her help. Since Mary is Queen and Mother of the Church, we present to her the needs of the Church throughout the world. We pray that the peace and joy which fills the kingdom of heaven may somehow be extended to us on earth. We pray that with Mary's assistance, God's kingdom may come, and that God's will may be done on earth as it is in heaven.

MORNING STAR

Pope John Paul encourages us to see Mary as the Morning Star who announces the coming of Christ into our world. Mary was the Morning Star two thousand years ago when she conceived and gave birth to Jesus. She has been the Morning Star throughout history, directing humanity to her son. As we grow in our understanding of her role as Mother of Jesus and Mother of the Church, Mary is a Morning Star giving us hope and light. She will be a Morning Star at the moment of our death.

"Hail, holy Queen....After this our exile, show unto us the blessed fruit of your womb, Jesus!"

Questions for Discussion and Reflection

What do you think heaven will be like? What will you talk about in your first conversation with Mary?

Can you explain how the rosary is a prayer that brings people closer to Jesus? What part does Mary play in this?

We should think often about the incredible mystery of the Incarnation, God becoming one of us. We should ponder the greatest act of love in history, Christ's passion and death. We should consider the miracle of Christ's Resurrection, and our own final goal, heaven. Who is more likely to meditate on these grace-events on a regular basis, someone who prays the rosary or someone who does not? Does this explain why the rosary has become such a popular Christian prayer?

Activities

Find a quiet place to pray. Picture the moment of your death. Mary has heard your request that she pray for you at the hour of your death. She welcomes you and brings you into the presence of Jesus. Consider the joy of finally being home with God, where there are no more fears, no suffering, but only endless joy and peace with Jesus, Mary, the angels, the saints, and your loved ones. Thank Mary for being your Mother. Thank Jesus for being your Savior, your Lord, and your God.

BIBLIOGRAPHY

Abbott, Walter, editor. *The Documents of Vatican II.* New York: Herder and Herder, 1966.

Book of Blessings. International Committee on English in the Liturgy, Washington, D.C.: United States Catholic Conference, 1988.

Brown, R.E., K.P. Donfried, J.A. Fitzmeyer, J. Reumann, editors. *Mary in the New Testament.* New York: Paulist Press, 1978.

Carrel, Alexis. *The Voyage to Lourdes.* New York: Harper, 1950.

Catechism of the Catholic Church. Washington, D.C.: United States Catholic Conference, 1994.

Collection of Masses of the Blessed Virgin Mary. Volume 1: *Sacramentary.* Volume 2: *Lectionary.* New York: Catholic Book Publishing Company, 1992.

Cranston, Ruth. *The Miracle of Lourdes.* New York: McGraw Hill Book Company, 1955.

Dictionary of Mary. New York: Catholic Book Publishing Company, 1985.

Groeschel, Benedict. *A Still, Small Voice: A Practical Guide on Reported Revelations.* San Francisco: Ignatius Press, 1993.

Houselander, Caryll. *The Reed of God.* Westminster, MD: Christian Classics, Inc. 1985.

John Paul II. *Mother of the Redeemer.* Boston, MA: Daughters of Saint Paul, 1987.

Lukefahr, Oscar. *A Catholic Guide to the Bible.* Liguori, MO: Liguori Publications, 1992.

_____. *The Privilege of Being Catholic.* Liguori, MO: Liguori Publications, 1993.

_____. *"We Believe..." A Survey of the Catholic Faith.* Revised and Cross-Referenced to the *Catechism of the Catholic Church,* Liguori, MO: Liguori Publications, 1995.

Montague, George T. *Our Father, Our Mother: Mary and the Faces of God.* Steubenville, OH: Franciscan University Press, 1990.

New Catholic Encyclopedia. New York: McGraw-Hill Book Company, 1967.

New Revised Standard Version of the Bible. New York: Division of Christian Education of the National Council of the Churches of Christ in the USA, 1989.

O'Carroll, Michael. *Theotokos: A Theological Encyclopedia of the Blessed Virgin Mary.* Wilmington, DE: Michael Glazier, Inc., 1982.

Tanquerey, Adolphe. *The Spiritual Life.* Desclee and Company, Tournai, Belgium. 1932.

Vawter, Bruce. *Revelation: A Divine Message of Hope.* New Haven, CT: Knights of Columbus.

Ward, J. Neville. *Five for Sorrow, Ten for Joy: A Consideration of the Rosary.* Revised Edition. Cambridge, MA: Cowley Publications, 1985.

INDEX